Principles
in Practice

MW01130910

The Principles in Practice imprint offers teachers concrete illustrations of effective classroom practices based in NCTE research briefs and policy statements. Each book discusses the research on a specific topic, links the research to an NCTE brief or policy statement, and then demonstrates how those principles come alive in practice: by showcasing actual classroom practices that demonstrate the policies in action; by talking about research in practical, teacher-friendly language; and by offering teachers possibilities for rethinking their own practices in light of the ideas presented in the books. Books within the imprint are grouped in strands, each strand focused on a significant topic of interest.

Adolescent Literacy Strand

Adolescent Literacy at Risk? The Impact of Standards (2009) Rebecca Bowers Sipe

Adolescents and Digital Literacies: Learning Alongside Our Students (2010) Sara Kajder

Adolescent Literacy and the Teaching of Reading: Lessons for Teachers of Literature (2010) Deborah Appleman

Rethinking the "Adolescent" in Adolescent Literacy (2017) Sophia Tatiana Sarigianides, Robert Petrone, and Mark A. Lewis

Restorative Justice in the English Language Arts Classroom (2019) Maisha T. Winn, Hannah Graham, and Rita Renjitham Alfred

Writing in Today's Classrooms Strand

Writing in the Dialogical Classroom: Students and Teachers Responding to the Texts of Their Lives (2011) Bob Fecho

Becoming Writers in the Elementary Classroom: Visions and Decisions (2011) Katie Van Sluys

Writing Instruction in the Culturally Relevant Classroom (2011) Maisha T. Winn and Latrise P. Johnson

Writing Can Change Everything: Middle Level Kids Writing Themselves into the World (2020) Shelbie Witte, editor

Growing Writers: Principles for High School Writers and Their Teachers (2021) Anne Elrod Whitney

Literacy Assessment Strand

Our Better Judgment: Teacher Leadership for Writing Assessment (2012) Chris W. Gallagher and Eric D. Turley

Beyond Standardized Truth: Improving Teaching and Learning through Inquiry-Based Reading Assessment (2012) Scott Filkins

Reading Assessment: Artful Teachers, Successful Students (2013) Diane Stephens, editor

Going Public with Assessment: A Community Practice Approach (2018) Kathryn Mitchell Pierce and Rosario Ordoñez-Jasis

Literacies of the Disciplines Strand

Entering the Conversations: Practicing Literacy in the Disciplines (2014) Patricia Lambert Stock, Trace Schillinger, and Andrew Stock

Real-World Literacies: Disciplinary Teaching in the High School Classroom (2014) Heather Lattimer

Doing and Making Authentic Literacies (2014) Linda Denstaedt, Laura Jane Roop, and Stephen Best

Reading in Today's Classrooms Strand

Connected Reading: Teaching Adolescent Readers in a Digital World (2015) Kristen Hawley Turner and Troy Hicks

Digital Reading: What's Essential in Grades 3–8 (2015) William L. Bass II and Franki Sibberson

Teaching Reading with YA Literature: Complex Texts, Complex Lives (2016) Jennifer Buehler

Teaching English Language Learners Strand

Beyond "Teaching to the Test": Rethinking Accountability and Assessment for English Language Learners (2017) Betsy Gilliland and Shannon Pella

Community Literacies en Confianza: Learning from Bilingual After-School Programs (2017) Steven Alvarez

Understanding Language: Supporting ELL Students in Responsive ELA Classrooms (2017) Melinda J. McBee Orzulak

Writing across Culture and Language: Inclusive Strategies for Working with ELL Writers in the ELA Classroom (2017) Christina Ortmeier-Hooper

Students' Rights to Read and Write Strand

Adventurous Thinking: Fostering Students' Rights to Read and Write in Secondary ELA Classrooms (2019) Mollie V. Blackburn, editor

In the Pursuit of Justice: Students' Rights to Read and Write in Elementary School (2020) Mariana Souto-Manning, editor

Already Readers and Writers: Honoring Students' Rights to Read and Write in the Middle Grade Classroom (2020) Jennifer Ochoa, editor

Growing Writers

Principles for High School Writers and Their Teachers

Anne Elrod Whitney
Pennsylvania State University

National Council of Teachers of English
340 N. Neil St., Suite #104, Champaign, Illinois 61820
www.ncte.org

Staff Editor: Bonny Graham
Imprint Editor: Cathy Fleischer
Interior Design: Victoria Pohlmann
Cover Design: Pat Mayer
Cover Image: Marvin Young, NCTE Visual and Member Communications Coordinator

NCTE Stock Number: 19174; eStock Number: 19181
ISBN 978-0-8141-1917-4; eISBN 978-0-8141-1918-1

Library of Congress Cataloging-in-Publication Data
Names: Whitney, Anne Elrod, author.
Title: Growing writers : principles for high school writers and their teachers / Anne Elrod Whitney.
Description: Champaign, Illinois : National Council of Teachers of English, 2021. | Series: Principles in practice | Includes bibliographical references and index. | Summary: "Explores how the principles defined in NCTE's "Professional Knowledge for the Teaching of Writing" position statement can support high school writers and teachers of writing; principles help us better understand our teaching purposes, make decisions about teaching, vet ideas supplied by others, and grow as teachers of writing"—Provided by publisher.
Identifiers: LCCN 2021008676 (print) | LCCN 2021008677 (ebook) | ISBN 9780814119174 (trade paperback) | ISBN 9780814119181 (adobe pdf)
Subjects: LCSH: English language—Composition and exercises—Study and teaching (Secondary) | Composition (Language arts)—Study and teaching (Secondary)
Classification: LCC LB1631 .W3824 2021 (print) | LCC LB1631 (ebook) | DDC 808/.0420712—dc23
LC record available at https://lccn.loc.gov/2021008676
LC ebook record available at https://lccn.loc.gov/2021008677

To high school writers: you inherit a world so damaged but still with such potential. May writing lift your voices and nourish your souls.

To their teachers: it matters.

Contents

Acknowledgments

It was Sheridan Blau, my academic father, who taught me that magic always happens once teachers of writing get down to real talk and writing of their own. Thank you for your love, your example, and your indefatigable ability to become interested.

What might the life of teaching writing be like without the National Council of Teachers of English and the National Writing Project? The people of these two organizations are living proof that we are better together than any one of us can be on our own. Thank you for keeping our flame.

The contributing authors whose chapters appear in this book must be the most patient writers on the earth. Thank you for sharing not only your teaching practice but also your vulnerability—and your grace with my own.

This book grew into being during a time of unbelievable tumult in the world and in my own life. There would not be a book at all without the loving attention of Cathy Fleischer, mentor and imprint editor. From the initial idea for the book to its completion, across all boundaries from the writing to the world around us to my own spirit, Cathy lovingly held my hand and kept her faith in me. I am grateful.

Professional Knowledge for the Teaching of Writing

Approved in February 2016, this revised statement replaces the *NCTE Beliefs about the Teaching of Writing* (November 2004), now sunsetted.

A subcommittee of the NCTE Executive Committee wrote the *NCTE Beliefs about the Teaching of Writing* in 2004. In over a decade since, the everyday experience of writing in people's lives has expanded dramatically. Increasingly, handheld devices are important instruments for people's writing, integrated tightly, nearly seamlessly, with their composing in video, photographs, and other media. Geographic location and embodied presence have become more salient to writing than at most times in human history. The ways writing and the spoken voice are mutually supportive in writing processes have become increasingly facilitated by technological capabilities. Globalized economies and relative ease of transportation have continued to bring languages into contact with one another, and US educational scholars and, sometimes, institutions have made progress in considering what it means for individuals to be adding new written languages to existing ones. Even as these expansions have enlarged the experience of writing outside school, implementation of the first USA nationwide standards in literacy—the Common Core State Standards—has, in some places, contributed to narrowing students' experience of writing inside school. In that contradictory and shifting environment, the NCTE Executive Committee charged a committee to update the *Beliefs about the Teaching of Writing*, attempting to reflect some of the historically significant changes of recent years. What follows are some of the professional principles that guide effective teaching.

Writing grows out of many purposes.

Writing is not just one practice or activity. A note to a cousin is not like a business report, which is different again from a poem. The processes and ways of thinking that lead to these varied kinds of texts can also vary widely, from the quick email to a friend to the careful drafting and redrafting of a legal contract. The different purposes and genres both grow out of and create varied relationships between the writers and the readers, and existing relationships are reflected in degrees of formality in language, as well as assumptions about what knowledge and experience are already shared, and what needs to be explained. Writing with certain purposes in mind, the writer focuses attention on what the audience is thinking or believing; other times, the writer focuses more on the information she or he is organizing, or on her or his own emergent thoughts and feelings. Therefore, the thinking, procedures, and physical format in writing are shaped in accord with the author's purpose(s), the needs of the audience, and the conventions of the genre.

Often, in school, students write only to prove that they did something they were asked to do, in order to get credit for it. Or, students are taught a single type of writing and are led to believe this type will suffice in all situations. Since writers outside school have many different purposes beyond demonstrating accountability and they use more diverse genres

Professional Knowledge for the Teaching of Writing

of writing, it is important that students have experiences within school that teach them how writing differs with purpose, audience, and other elements of the situation. Even within more academic settings like college courses, the characteristics of good writing vary among disciplines; what counts as a successful lab report, for example, differs from a successful history paper, online discussion contribution, essay exam, reflection on service learning, or interpretative statement about a work of art.

Thus, beyond the traditional purposes that are identified in school, purposes for writing include developing social networks; reasoning with others to improve society; supporting personal and spiritual growth; reflecting on experience; communicating professionally and academically; building relationships with others, including friends, family, and like-minded individuals; and engaging in aesthetic experiences.

What does this mean for teaching?

In order to provide high-quality writing opportunities for all students, teachers need to understand

- The wide range of purposes for which people write and the different kinds of texts and processes that arise from those purposes;
- Strategies and forms for writing for public participation in a democratic society;
- Ways people use writing for personal growth, expression, and reflection, and how to encourage and develop this kind of writing;
- How people make creative and literary texts, aesthetic genres, for the purposes of entertainment, pleasure, or exploration;
- The ways digital environments have added new modalities while constantly creating new publics, audiences, purposes, and invitations to compose;
- The range of non-public uses of writing for self-organization, reflection, planning, and management of information, and the many tools, digital and otherwise, that people use for these purposes;
- Appropriate genres for varied academic disciplines and the purposes and relationships that create those forms;
- Ways of organizing and transforming school curricula in order to provide students with adequate education in varied purposes for writing;
- How to set up a course that asks students to write for varied purposes and audiences.

Related:
Writing Now: A Policy Research Brief Produced by the National Council of Teachers of English [1]

Writing is embedded in complex social relationships and their appropriate languages.

Writing happens in the midst of a web of relationships. Most clearly, the relationship between the writer and the reader can be very specific: writers often have a definite idea of who will read their work, not just a generalized notion that their text will be available to the

Professional Knowledge for the Teaching of Writing

world. Furthermore, particular people surround the writer—other writers, friends, members of a given community—during the process of composing. They may know what the writer is doing and be indirectly involved in it, though they are not the audience for the work. In workplace and academic settings, writers often write because someone in authority tells them to. Therefore, power relationships are built into the writing situation. In every writing situation, the writer, the reader, and all relevant others live in a structured social order, where some people's words count more than others, where being heard is more difficult for some people than others, where some people's words come true and others' do not.

Writers start in different places. It makes a difference what kinds of language writers spoke while growing up and may speak at home now, and how those experiences relate to the kinds of language they are being asked to take when composing. It makes a difference, too, the culture a writer comes from, the ways people use language in that culture and the degree to which that culture is privileged in the larger society. Important cultural differences are not only linguistic but also racial, economic, geographic, and ideological. Digital environments have created new contexts in which new languages are being invented continuously, and young people are often leading innovators of "digitalk." The Internet brings global languages into contact, even as it provides new contexts for each language—written and oral—to change.

What does this mean for teaching?

The teaching of writing should assume students will begin with the language with which they are most at home and most fluent in their speech. That language may be a variety of English or a different language altogether. The languages students learn first are the bedrock upon which all other language traditions and forms will be constructed. The ultimate goal is not to leave students where they are, however, but to move them toward greater flexibility, so that they can write not just for their own intimates but for wider audiences. Teachers will want to engage in respectful inquiry with students about significant differences between patterns in their use of their first language and more conventionally written English. Even as they move toward more widely used English, writers find that it is not necessary or desirable to eliminate the ways their family and people in their neighborhood use words to express themselves. The teaching of excellence in writing means adding language to what already exists, not subtracting. Further, expert writing teachers deliberately teach students to incorporate their heritage and home languages intentionally and strategically in the texts they write. The goal is to make more relationships available, not fewer.

In order to provide high-quality writing opportunities for all students, teachers need to understand:

- How to find out about students' language use in the home and their neighborhoods, the changes in language context they may have encountered in their lives, and the kinds of language they most value;
- The ways wider social situations in which students speak, write, read, and relate to other people affect what feels to them natural or unnatural, easy or hard;

Professional Knowledge for the Teaching of Writing

- How mixing languages within a text can promote students' acquisition of academic language, deeper competence in a repertoire of codes, ability to communicate complex thoughts, and ways of communicating with various audiences;
- How teachers who do not speak or understand a student's home language can embrace and support the use of home languages in the classroom;
- How to discuss respectfully with students expectations for flexibility in the employment of different kinds of language for different social contexts in order to gain access to some powerful social worlds;
- How to help students negotiate maintenance of their most familiar and cherished language practices while developing strength in academic classroom English;
- Control and awareness of their own varied and strategic ways of using language and the social contexts that expect them;
- An understanding of the relationships among group affiliation, identity, and language;
- Knowledge of the usual patterns of common dialects in English, such as African American English, Spanish, and varieties of English related to Spanish, common patterns in American rural and urban populations, predictable patterns in the English varieties of groups common in their teaching contexts;
- The online spaces through which students communicate, and how their uses of digitalk differs from conventional written English.

Related:
CCCC Statement on Second Language Writing and Writers [2]
Resolution on the Student's Right to Incorporate Heritage and Home Languages in Writing [3]

Composing occurs in different modalities and technologies.

Composing has always required technology, whether it's the technology we associate with print—including pens, pencils, and paper—or the technology we associate with the digital—including word processors, digital imaging software, and the Internet. Like all texts, print texts are multimodal: print, whether hand-created or machine-produced, relies for meaning on multiple modalities, including language, layout, and the visual characteristics of the script. Moreover, print has often included visuals—including maps, line drawings, illustrations, and graphs—to create a fuller representation of meaning, to tap the familiarity of a visual to help readers make meaning in a new genre, to add aesthetic value, and to appeal to a wider audience. Film, television, and video involve such combinations of modalities, as do presentation software and websites. As technologies for composing have expanded, "composing" has increasingly referred to a suite of activities in varied modalities. Composers today work with many modalities, including language, layout, still images, other visuals, video, and sound. Computers, both the stationary and mobile varieties, provide a work environment where composers can employ and combine these modalities. Moreover, the Internet not only makes a range of new and diverse materials available to writers, but also brings writers and readers closer together and makes possible new kinds of collabora-

Professional Knowledge for the Teaching of Writing

tions. Thus, when students have access to a computer with full Internet access, composing opportunities expand.

Additionally, increased access to various modalities and technologies has created opportunities for students with a wide range of abilities, backgrounds, and languages to compose with more independence and agency. As more digital tools become available, and more forms of expression are not only accepted but expected, more students are able to employ these tools independently.

What does this mean for teaching?

Writing instruction should support students as they compose with a variety of modalities and technologies. Because students will, in the wider world, be using word processing for drafting, revision, and editing, incorporating visual components in some compositions, and including links where appropriate, definitions of composing should include these practices; definitions that exclude them are out-of-date and inappropriate.

Because many teachers and students do not have access to the most up-to-date technologies, such as portable devices with cameras, teaching students to compose multimodally may best be accomplished by foregrounding multimodal dimensions of composing in low-tech environments. An assignment for students to create picture books, for example, can allow them to consider how languages and images complement each other and assist the reader. Similar kinds of visual/verbal thinking can be supported across the school curriculum through other illustrated text forms, including journals, design notebooks, and posters. Attention to modalities in assignments and genres like these demonstrates the extent to which "new" literacies are rooted in older ones.

In order to provide high-quality writing opportunities for all students, teachers need to understand:

- A range of new genres that have emerged on the Internet;
- Open-source platforms that students can use for composing and electronic portfolios;
- Design and layout principles for print and digital publication;
- Conventions for digital communication, including email, chat, text messages, social networking, and online discussion forums;
- Ways to navigate both the World Wide Web and Web-based databases;
- Ways to access, evaluate, use, and cite information found on the Internet;
- Theory about and history of modalities, technologies, and the affordances they offer for meaning making;
- Operation of hardware and software that composers use, including resources for solving software and hardware problems;
- Tools that help students compose as independently as possible, in the modalities that best fit their needs and purposes;
- Internet resources for remaining up-to-date on technologies.

Professional Knowledge for the Teaching of Writing

Related:
Resolution on Composing with Nonprint Media [4]
Position Statement on Multimodal Literacies [5]
CCCC Position Statement on Teaching, Learning, and Assessing Writing in Digital Environments [6]
21st-Century Literacies: A Policy Research Brief [7]

Conventions of finished and edited texts are an important dimension of the relationship between writers and readers.

Readers expect writing to conform to their expectations. For public texts written for a general audience, contemporary readers expect words to be spelled in a standardized way, for punctuation to be used in predictable ways, for usage and syntax to match that used in texts they already acknowledged as successful. They expect the style in a piece of writing to be appropriate to its genre and social situation. With that in mind, writers try to use these surface elements strategically, in order to present the identity, create the relationships, and express the ideas that suit their purpose.

What does this mean for teaching?

Every teacher has to resolve a tension between writing as generating and shaping ideas and writing as a final product, demonstrating expected surface conventions. On the one hand, it is important for writing to be as correct as possible and for students to be able to produce correct texts so that readers can read and make meaning from them. On the other hand, achieving correctness is only one set of things writers must be able to do; a correct document empty of ideas or unsuited to its audience or purpose is not a good piece of writing. There is no formula for resolving this tension. Though it may be desirable both fluently to produce writing and to adhere to conventions, growth in fluency and control of conventions may not occur at the same time. If a student's mental energies are focused on new intellectual challenges, he or she may attend less fully to details of grammar and punctuation.

Such uneven development should be tolerated and, in fact, encouraged. Too much emphasis on correctness can actually inhibit a writer's development. By the same token, without mastering conventions for written discourse, writers may find their efforts regarded less highly by readers they had wanted to influence. Each teacher must be knowledgeable enough about the entire landscape of writing instruction to guide particular students toward a goal, including increasing fluency in new contexts, mastering conventions, and perhaps most important, developing rhetorical sophistication and appropriateness—all of which work together. NCTE's stated policy over many years has been that conventions of writing are best taught in the context of writing.

Most writing teachers teach students how to edit their writing that will be shared with audiences. This is often considered a late stage in the process of composing, because editing is only essential for the words, visuals, and other materials that are left after all the cutting, replacing, rewriting, and adding that go on during revision. Writers keep an image in their minds of conventional grammar, spelling, and punctuation in order to compare what is already on the page to what their audience expects. They also need to be aware of stylistic

Professional Knowledge for the Teaching of Writing

options and larger language choices that will best articulate their ideas and produce the most desirable impression on their readers. Language choices may be a matter of the identity a writer seeks to project, and those identities may not be productively standardized. In digital environments, there may be an expected way of using language due to the nature of the platform, such as in texting or blogging, where the conventional usage might differ from language in other contexts.

An area of consideration with respect to conventions in writing is the development of language proficiency for students learning English as an additional language. Experienced teachers understand that these multilingual students will enter the classroom at different stages and vary in the pace with which they acquire their new language. Knowledge of students' cultural and linguistic background and the way that background intersects or differs from English language conventions helps ensure that students are receiving instruction appropriate for their current stage of language learning. Writers who are learning English as an additional language will have multiple possible patterns in mind for phonology, morphology, syntax, and often genre and pragmatics as well. That is, they know more, and are sorting through that knowledge. Some may require support in analyzing the expectations of a wider English-dominant audience in contrast to the patterns of their earlier language(s). For many, patterns from the first language will persist and should be treated with the respect and generosity that should be afforded to spoken accented English.

In order to provide high-quality writing opportunities for all students, teachers need to understand:

- Developmental factors in writing, including the tension between fluency with new operations or content and the practices that produce accepted spelling, punctuation, syntactic, and usage conventions;
- Diverse influences and constraints on writers' decision making as they determine the conventions that apply to this situation and this piece of writing;
- A variety of applications and options for most conventions;
- Appropriate conventions for writing for a particular public audience;
- Linguistic terminology that is helpful for teaching particular kinds of usage without employing excessive linguistic terminology;
- Linguistic terminology helpful for communicating professionally with other educators;
- The relationship among rhetorical considerations and decisions about conventions, for example, the conditions under which a dash, a comma, a semicolon, or a full stop might be more effective;
- Conventions beyond the sentence, such as effective uses of bulleted lists, mixed genres and voices, diagrams and charts, design of pages, and composition of video shots;
- The conditions under which people learn to participate in new social situations, both personal and professional, with language;
- How to understand technologies such as grammar and spelling checkers to decide which changes are applicable in a given editing situation.

Professional Knowledge for the Teaching of Writing

Related:
Students' Right to Their Own Language [8]
CCCC Statement on Second Language Writers and Writing [2]

Everyone has the capacity to write; writing can be taught; and teachers can help students become better writers.

Developing writers require support. This support can best come through carefully designed writing instruction oriented toward acquiring new strategies and skills. Certainly, writers can benefit from teachers who simply support and give them time to write. However, high-quality instruction matters. Teachers of writing should be well versed in composition theory and research, and they should know methods for turning that theory into practice. They should be capable of teaching writing in both print and digital environments.

Students are different from one another, and they bring to the experience of writing a wide range of resources and strengths. At the same time, any writer can be positioned as weak, struggling, or incompetent. All writers need to learn multiple strategies and modalities to compensate for moments when they feel stuck or defeated, to get on with the business of composing.

As is the case with many activities, becoming a better writer requires that students write. This means actual writing for real audiences, not merely listening to lectures about writing, doing grammar drills, or discussing readings. The more people write, the more familiar it becomes and the more they are motivated to do it. Writers learn from each session with their hands on a keyboard or fingers on a pencil as they draft, rethink, revise, and draft again. Improvement is built into the experience of writing when writers revise, strategizing ways to make their writing better.

What does this mean for teaching?

Writing instruction must include ample in-class and out-of-class opportunities for writing, including writing in digital spaces, and should involve writing for a variety of purposes and audiences, including audiences beyond the classroom. Teachers need to support students in the development of writing lives, habits, and preferences for life outside school. We already know that many students do extensive amounts of self-sponsored writing: emailing, keeping journals or doing creative projects, instant messaging, making websites, blogging, creating fan fiction. Though critically important for college and career, the teaching of writing should also be geared toward making sense in a life outside of school, so that writing has ample room to grow in individuals' lives. It is useful for teachers to consider what elements of their curriculum they could imagine students self-sponsoring outside school. Ultimately, those are the activities that will produce more writing.

In order to provide high-quality writing opportunities for all students, teachers need to understand:

- How to interpret curriculum documents, including standards, skills, strategies, concepts, and content that can be taught while students are actually writing, rather than one dimension of composing at a time to all students at once;

Professional Knowledge for the Teaching of Writing

- How to create writing lives for the world beyond school;
- How to construct social structures that support independent work;
- How to confer with individual writers;
- How to assess students' work while they are in the process of writing—formatively—in order to offer timely assistance during the composing process;
- How to plan what students need to know in response to ongoing research;
- How to create a sense of community and personal safety in the classroom, so that students are willing to write and collaborate freely and at length;
- How to effectively employ a variety of technologies such as brainstorming tools, collaborative word processors, and bibliography managers for students to engage in writing fully;
- How to ensure that every student has the tools and supports necessary to be as independent as possible;
- How to encourage and include students writing in their home languages.

Related:
NCTE Beliefs about Students' Right to Write [9]
Resolution on Students' Right of Expression [10]
What We Know about Writing, Grades K–2 [11]
How to Help Your Child Become a Better Writer (English) [12]
How to Help Your Child Become a Better Writer (Español) [13]

Writing is a process.

Often, when people think of writing, they think of texts—finished pieces of writing that stand alone. Understanding what writers do, however, involves both thinking about what texts look like when they are finished as well as thinking about what strategies writers might employ to produce those texts, especially when using a variety of technologies. Knowledge about writing is only complete when writers understand the ensemble of actions in which they engage as they produce texts. Such understanding has two aspects, at least. First is the development, through extended practice over years, of a repertory of routines, skills, strategies, and practices, for generating, revising, and editing different kinds of texts. Second is the development of reflective abilities and meta-awareness about writing. The procedural knowledge developed through reflective practice helps writers most when they encounter difficulty, or when they are in the middle of creating a piece of writing. How does someone get started? What do they do when they get stuck? How do they plan the overall process, each section of their work, and even the rest of the sentence they are writing right now? Research, theory, and practice in the teaching of writing have produced a rich understanding of what writers do, those who are proficient and professional as well as those who struggle.

Two further points are vital. First, to say that writing is a process is decidedly not to say that it should—or can—be turned into a formulaic set of steps or reduced to a set of traits. Experienced writers shift between different operations according to their audience, the pur-

Professional Knowledge for the Teaching of Writing

pose of the writing task, the genre, and circumstances, such as deadlines and considerations of length, style, and format.

Second, writers do not accumulate process skills and strategies once and for all. They develop and refine writing skills throughout their writing lives, as they take up new tasks in new genres for new audiences. They grow continually, across personal and professional contexts, using numerous writing spaces and technologies.

What does this mean for teaching?

Whenever possible, teachers should attend to the process that students might follow to produce texts—and not only specify criteria for evaluating finished products, in form or content. Students should become comfortable with prewriting techniques, multiple strategies for developing and organizing a message, a variety of strategies for revising and editing, and methods for preparing products for public audiences and for deadlines. In explaining assignments, teachers should provide guidance and options for ways of accomplishing the objectives. Using formative assessment to understand the processes students follow—the decisions they make, the attempts along the way—can be at least as important as evaluating the final product with a holistic score or grade. Moreover, they should understand how various digital writing tools—mind mapping, word processing, bibliography managers—can be employed in academically useful ways. At least some of the time, the teacher should guide the students through the process, assisting them as they go. Writing instruction must provide opportunities for students to identify the processes that work best for themselves as they move from one initial idea to final draft, from one writing situation to another.

Writing instruction must also take into account that a good deal of workplace writing and other writing takes place in collaborative situations. Writers must learn to work effectively with one another to create writing, provide feedback, and complete a final draft, often with the use of collaborative technologies.

In order to provide high-quality writing opportunities for all students, teachers need to understand:

- The relationship between features of finished writing and the actions writers perform to create that writing;
- What writers of different genres, including political arguments, stories, poems, blog posts, technical reports, and more, say about their craft;
- The process of writing from the inside, that is, what the teachers themselves as writers experience in a host of different writing situations;
- Multiple strategies for approaching a wide range of typical problems writers face during composing, including strategies for invention, audience, and task analysis, incorporation of images and other visuals, revision, and editing;
- Multiple, flexible models of the writing process, the varied ways individuals approach similar tasks, and the ways that writing situations and genres inform processes;
- How to design time and possibly staged intervals of work for students to do their best work on a given assignment;

Professional Knowledge for the Teaching of Writing

- A range of digital writing tools that writers might find useful in their processes, including word processors, databases, outliners, mind mapping software, design software, shared-document websites, and other hardware, software, and Web-based technologies.

Related:
Framework for Success in Postsecondary Writing [14]
CCCC Principles for the Postsecondary Teaching of Writing [15]

Writing is a tool for thinking.

When writers actually write, they think of things that they did not have in mind before they began writing. The act of writing generates ideas; writing can be an act of discovery. This is different from the way we often think of writers—as the solitary author who works diligently to get ideas fixed in his or her head before writing them down. The notion that writing is a medium for thought is important in several ways and suggests a number of important uses for writing: to solve problems, to identify issues, to construct questions, to reconsider something one had already figured out, to try out a half-baked idea. This insight that writing is a tool for thinking helps us to understand the process of drafting and revision as one of exploration, and is nothing like the idea of writing as transcribing from prerecorded tape. Nor is the writing process simply fixing the mistakes in an early draft; rather, it involves finding more and more wrinkles and implications in what one is talking about.

What does this mean for teaching?

In any writing classroom, some of the writing is for the writer and some for other audiences as well. Regardless of the age, ability, or experience of the writer, the use of writing to generate thought is still valuable; therefore, forms of writing such as personal narrative, journals, written reflections, observations, and writing-to-learn strategies should be included in the curriculum.

In order to provide high-quality writing opportunities for all students, teachers need to understand:

- How to employ varied tools for thinking through writing, such as journals, writers' notebooks, blogs, sketchbooks, digital portfolios, listservs or online discussion groups, dialogue journals, double-entry or dialectical journals, and others;
- The kinds of new thinking—such as questioning, discovery, and invention—that occur when writers revise;
- The varieties of thinking people do when they compose, and what those types of thinking look like when they appear in writing;
- Strategies for getting started with an idea, or finding an idea when one does not occur immediately;
- Exploring various technologies such as drawing tools and voice-to-text translators for brainstorming and developing one's initial thinking;

Professional Knowledge for the Teaching of Writing

- Ways to accommodate differences among students, such as those who find writing physically challenging, by using oral rehearsal of ideas, gesture, diagramming, or other options that would still allow exploration and development of thought.

Related:
Resolution on Writing Across the Curriculum [16]

Writing has a complex relationship to talk.

From its beginnings in early childhood, through K–2 and college classrooms, and throughout a variety of workplaces and community settings, writing exists in an environment of talk. Speakers often write notes or scripts. Writers often talk in order to rehearse the language and content that will go into what they write, and conversation often provides an impetus or occasion for writing. Writers sometimes confer with teachers and other writers about what to do next, how to improve their drafts, or how to clarify their ideas and purposes. Their usual ways of speaking either may or may not feed into the sentences they write, depending on intricate, continuous, important decisions.

What does this mean for teaching?

In early childhood, teachers expect lots of talk to surround writing, since children are figuring out how to get speech onto paper. Early teaching in composition should also attend to helping children get used to producing language orally, through telling stories, explaining how things work, predicting what will happen, and guessing about why things and people are the way they are. Early writing experiences will often include students explaining orally what is in a text, whether it is printed or drawn.

As they grow, writers still need opportunities to talk about what they are writing about, to rehearse the language of their upcoming texts and run ideas by trusted colleagues before and as they take the risk of committing words to paper. After making a draft, it is often helpful for writers to discuss with peers what they have done, partly in order to get ideas from their peers, partly to see what they, the writers, say when they try to explain their thinking. Writing conferences, wherein student writers talk about their work with a teacher, who can make suggestions or reorient what the writer is doing, are also very helpful uses of talk in the writing process.

In order to provide high-quality writing opportunities for all students, teachers need to understand:

- Ways of setting up and managing student talk in partnerships and groups;
- Ways of establishing a balance between talk and writing in classroom management;
- Ways of organizing the classroom and/or schedule to permit individual teacher-student conferences;
- Strategies for deliberate insertions of opportunities for talk into the writing process: knowing when and how students should talk about their writing;
- Ways of anticipating and solving interpersonal conflicts that arise when students discuss writing;

Professional Knowledge for the Teaching of Writing

- Relationships—both similarities and differences—between oral and literate language;
- The uses of writing in public presentations and the values of students making oral presentations that grow out of and use their writing;
- How technologies such as voice recording apps on smartphones and audio editing tools can be used as students create podcasts, videos, or other multimedia work in which they share their writing through oral production.

Related:
What We Know about Writing, Grades 3–5 [17]
What We Know about Writing, Grades 6–8 [18]

Writing and reading are related.

Writing and reading are related. People who engage in considerable reading often find writing an easier task, though the primary way a writer improves is through writing. Still, it's self-evident that to write a particular kind of text, it helps if the writer has read that kind of text, if only because the writer then has a mental model of the genre. In order to take on a particular style of language, it also helps to have read that language, to have heard it in one's mind, so that one can hear it again in order to compose it.

Writing can also help people become better readers. In their earliest writing experiences, children listen for the relationships of sounds to letters, which contributes greatly to their phonemic awareness and phonics knowledge. Writers also must learn how texts are structured, because eventually they have to compose in different genres, and that knowledge of structure helps them to predict and make sense of the sections and sequencing of the texts they read. The experience of plotting a short story, organizing a research report, or making line breaks in a poem permits the writer, as a reader, to approach new reading experiences with more informed eyes.

Additionally, reading is a vital source of information and ideas. For writers fully to contribute to a given topic or to be effective in a given situation, they must be familiar with and draw on what previous writers have said. Reading also creates a sense of what one's audience knows or expects on a topic.

What does this mean for teaching?

One way teachers help students become better writers is to make sure they have lots of extended time to read, in school and out. Teachers also make sure students have access to and experience in reading material that presents both professionally published and student writing in various genres. If one is going to write in a genre, it is very helpful to have read in that genre first.

Overall, frequent conversations about the connections between what we read and what we write are helpful. These connections will sometimes be about the structure and craft of the writing itself, and sometimes about thematic and content connections.

In order to provide high-quality writing opportunities for all students, teachers need to understand:

Professional Knowledge for the Teaching of Writing

- How writers read for the purposes of writing—with an eye toward not just what the text says but also how it is put together;
- The psychological and social processes reading and writing have in common;
- The ways writers imagine their intended readers, anticipating their responses and needs;
- That text structures are fluid enough to accommodate frequent exceptions, innovations, and disruptions;
- How writers can identify mentor or exemplar texts, both print and digital, that they may want to emulate in their own writing.

Related:
On Reading, Learning to Read, and Effective Reading Instruction [19]
Reading and Writing Across the Curriculum: A Policy Research Brief [20]
Framework for Success in Postsecondary Writing [21]

Assessment of writing involves complex, informed, human judgment.

Assessment of writing occurs for different purposes. The most fundamental and important assessment of writing is that of the writer, whose efficacy and growth demands that she or he determine and intend what to work on next, throughout the process of producing a single text and across experiences as she or he grows through a writing life. Sometimes, a teacher assesses in order to decide what the student has achieved and what he or she still needs to learn. Sometimes, an agency or institution beyond the classroom assesses a student's level of achievement in order to say whether he or she can go on to some new educational level that requires the writer to be able to do certain things. At other times, school authorities require a writing test as a mechanism for requiring teachers to teach writing, or a certain kind or genre of writing. Still other times, as in a history or literature exam, the assessment of writing itself is not the point, but the quality of the writing is evaluated almost in passing.

In any of these assessments of writing, complex judgments are required. Human beings need to make these judgments, not software programmed to score essays, because only human beings can be sensitive enough to purposes, audience, quality and relevance of evidence, truth in content, and the like. Furthermore, such judgments should be made by professionals who are educated and informed about writing, writing development, the various ways writing can be assessed, and the ways such assessments can support writers.

Instructors of composition should know about various methods of assessment of student writing. Instructors must recognize the difference between formative and summative evaluation and be prepared to evaluate students' writing from both perspectives. By formative evaluation here, we mean provisional, ongoing, in-process judgments about what students know and what to teach next—assessments that may be complex descriptions and not reduced to a grade or score and that are intended to support students' writerly development. By summative evaluation, we mean final judgments about the quality of student work (typically reflected in a grade).

In order to provide high-quality writing opportunities for all students, teachers need to understand:

Professional Knowledge for the Teaching of Writing

- How to find out what student writers can do, informally, on an ongoing basis;
- How to use that assessment in order to decide what and how to teach next;
- How to assess occasionally, less frequently, in order to form and report judgments about the quality of student writing and learning;
- How to assess ability and knowledge across multiple different writing engagements;
- What the features of good writing are, appropriate to the context and purposes of the teaching and learning;
- What the elements of a constructive process of writing are, appropriate to the context and purposes of the teaching and learning;
- What growth in writing looks like, the developmental aspects of writing ability;
- Ways of assessing student metacognitive process as they connect writing to reading;
- How to recognize in student writing (in both their texts and their actions) the nascent potential for excellence at the features and processes desired;
- How to deliver useful feedback, appropriate for the writer and the situation;
- How to analyze writing situations for their most essential elements, so that assessment is not of everything about writing all at once, but rather is targeted to outcomes;
- How to analyze and interpret both qualitative and quantitative writing assessments and make decisions about their usefulness;
- How to evaluate electronic texts;
- How to use portfolios to assist writers in their development and how to assess portfolios;
- How self-assessment and reflection contribute to a writer's development and ability to move among genres, media, and rhetorical situations;
- How to employ a variety of technologies—including screencasting and annotation, embedded text and voice comments, and learning management systems—to provide timely, useful, and goal-oriented feedback to students.

Related:

Writing Assessment: A Position Statement of CCCC [22]
NCTE Position Statement on Machine Scoring [23]
NCTE Resolution on Grading Student Writing [24]

Article printed from NCTE: **https://ncte.org**
URL to article: **https://ncte.org/statement/teaching-writing/**
URLs in this post:
[1] *Writing Now: A Policy Research Brief Produced by the National Council of Teachers of English*: **https://secure.ncte.org/library/NCTEFiles/Resources/Journals/CC/0181-sept2008/CC0181Policy.pdf**
[2] *CCCC Statement on Second Language Writing and Writers*: **https://cccc.ncte.org/cccc/resources/positions/secondlangwriting**

Professional Knowledge for the Teaching of Writing

[3] *Resolution on the Student's Right to Incorporate Heritage and Home Languages in Writing*: **https://ncte.org/statement/homelanguages/**

[4] *Resolution on Composing with Nonprint Media*: **https://ncte.org/statement/compose withnonprint/**

[5] *Position Statement on Multimodal Literacies*: **https://ncte.org/statement/multimodal literacies/**

[6] *CCCC Position Statement on Teaching, Learning, and Assessing Writing in Digital Environments*: **https://cccc.ncte.org/cccc/resources/positions/digitalenvironments**

[7] *21st-Century Literacies: A Policy Research Brief*: **https://secure.ncte.org/library/ NCTEFiles/Resources/Positions/Chron1107ResearchBrief.pdf**

[8] *Students' Right to Their Own Language*: **https://cccc.ncte.org/cccc/resources/positions/ srtolsummary**

[9] *NCTE Beliefs about Students' Right to Write*: **https://ncte.org/statement/students-right-to-write/**

[10] *Resolution on Students' Right of Expression*: **https://ncte.org/statement/rightof expression/**

[11] What We Know about Writing, Grades K–2: **http://www.ncte.org/writing/ aboutearlygrades**

[12]* *How to Help Your Child Become a Better Writer (English)*: **https://ncte.org/statement/ howtohelpenglish/**

[13] *How to Help Your Child Become a Better Writer (Español)*: **https://ncte.org/statement/ howtohelpspanish/**

[14] *Framework for Success in Postsecondary Writing*: **http://wpacouncil.org/framework**

[15] *CCCC Principles for the Postsecondary Teaching of Writing*: **https://cccc.ncte.org/cccc/ resources/positions/postsecondarywriting#principle5**

[16] *Resolution on Writing Across the Curriculum*: **https://www2.ncte.org/statement/ writingacrossthecurr/**

[17] *What We Know about Writing, Grades 3–5*: **http://www.ncte.org/writing/aboutelem**

[18] *What We Know about Writing, Grades 6–8*: **http://www.ncte.org/writing/aboutmiddle**

[19] *On Reading, Learning to Read, and Effective Reading Instruction*: **https://ncte.org/ statement/onreading/**

[20] *Reading and Writing Across the Curriculum: A Policy Research Brief*: **https://secure.ncte .org/library/NCTEFiles/Resources/Journals/CC/0203-mar2011/CC0203Policy.pdf**

[21] *Framework for Success in Postsecondary Writing*: **http://wpacouncil.org/files/frame work-for-success-postsecondary-writing.pdf**

[22] *Writing Assessment: A Position Statement of CCCC*: **https://cccc.ncte.org/cccc/resources/ positions/writingassessment**

[23] *NCTE Position Statement on Machine Scoring*: **https://ncte.org/statement/machine_ scoring/**

[24] *NCTE Resolution on Grading Student Writing*: **https://ncte.org/statement/grading studentwrit/**

*This resource was revised in 2018 and is now titled *Parents as Partners in Promoting Writing among Children and Youth*. The original URL is still good.

1 Professional Knowledge for the Teaching of Writing

Thinking about Professional Knowledge: Grounding Practice in Principles

Why This Book? The Case for Principles

"He who floats with the current, who does not guide himself according to higher principles, who has no ideal, no convictions—such a man is a mere article of the world's furniture—a thing moved, instead of a living and moving being—an echo, not a voice," wrote nineteenth-century Swiss philosopher Henri Frédéric Amiel in his journal (1885, p. 209). Isn't it so for teachers of writing? Teaching can sometimes feel like floating on a sea of approaches, philosophies, curricula, strategies, policies, and reforms. So many stakeholders have opinions about our work: it seems like every year or two, either *Newsweek*, the *New Yorker,* or the *Atlantic* chooses to run a piece or series with the words *writing crisis* in the title. At social gatherings, when I tell people I teach writing, they tell me how poorly kids write today, or how poorly adults do, and they have strong opinions about what we (I!) ought to be doing differently to fix it (mostly, teach more grammar). States institute writing standards and writing tests, revise them and/ or repeal them, then institute new ones in a cyclical fashion. And in schools, it's common for a new curriculum to be adopted or a new resource to be purchased, to have an initial burst of professional development around it, and then move on to something else just as quickly. All of these ideas about how to teach writing swirl around like foam on the waves, and if we're not paying attention, we writing teachers can find ourselves bobbing along without direction of our own or, worse, swept up in currents that take our writing instruction in directions we never meant to go.

This book is about centering our teaching on principles. The imprint of which it is a part, called Principles in Practice, expresses both an aspiration and a truth: first, an aspiration that teaching practice can be grounded in principle, centered on ideas that cohere and guide decision making; second, the truth that it is also possible to find ourselves engaging in practice that is just practice: doing things without knowing why we are doing them, or doing things that, though they "work," can also undermine what we are really trying to do with writers in the long term.

Principles Ground and Focus Our Selection and Adaptation of Practices

I entered the teaching profession with a strong grounding in teaching writing as process, in workshop-organized writing classrooms in which students would choose what to work on and direct themselves through drafting and revision at their own pace, and in which teaching any genre would begin with organic study of actual pieces of writing in that genre. I had learned these principles through university coursework, interaction with teachers who had been connected to the National Writing Project, and deep reading in the professional literature of our field—books like this one, most of which I had found in the shelves of my college library during slow hours at my tutoring job in the writing center. One thing I KNEW I would not do was assign a five-paragraph essay. I would not have students write essays for an unnamed (teacher) reader, either. And I DEFINITELY would not proffer a one-page template for essay planning. What if students' arguments contained more than one main point? What if they had fewer or more than three reasons, or if the reasons students had to offer for their claims were layered, varying in importance, or drawing on different sources of evidence? Nope, I would not do it.

Then, of course, I did it. While I did also teach in many of the ways I had hoped I would, after exactly one year I found myself handing out a photocopied essay template I had borrowed from a seasoned colleague. I had started having "timed essays" many Fridays, though not every Friday, like my colleague next door. And I had a poster on my wall, adapted from materials from Jane Schaffer, advising students that an essay paragraph should contain a just-so prescribed ratio of "TS, CDs, CMs, and CS"—that is, a formulaic recipe of Topic Sentence, Concrete Details, Commentary, and Concluding Statements.

Why do we so often do what we wished we never would, or find ourselves teaching in ways that openly clash with some of our dearest held teaching values? My values as a teacher had not changed, nor had my students become more needy or less skilled as writers. The truth was that there were things in those materials that my students and I needed: scaffolding for structuring arguments, tools for planning, and so on. We do first with support what we will later do on our own. As experienced adult writers, we can see how one might start with a formula provided by another, then quickly break the tool and go off on our own when our needs as arguers call for something different. Yet, when I photocopied and handed out worksheets in which students could basically fill in the blanks and produce a cookie-cutter essay, I know I wasn't helping students to work at that level of nuance. Instead, I left my students with two conflicting bases for action as writers: one that said writing was developing a form in light of your own purpose and your audience's needs, and another that said, "Here; fill out this form."

Even the very best teachers I know have had times like these—times when practices that "work" to teach a particular skill don't work together, or don't fit into the broader vision we have for students. Or times when, after using a strategy or making an assignment again and again over time, we lose the reasons *why* we do a thing and find ourselves doing it because, well, that's what we do in English 9. Also, if you like employment, there are times you have to go with the flow, right?

What I've discovered over time is that there is a place for those essay-writing supports in my writing instruction, but because I had not examined them thoughtfully in light of the principles I had identified as important, I wasn't able to bring to students that relationship between the help of the scaffold in the near term and the longer-term project of becoming an adaptive, flexible writer with skills to acquire new genres. Some of this was about me, but more of it was about the way my own principles sometimes—or often—seemed at odds with those held by others around me, and almost always at odds with those my school, the district, textbook publishers, or government entities were expressing. In situations where I cared most about students communicating, some other influence made it about achieving. Or when I cared most about emotions, some other structural frame foregrounded skills. Frankly, few of the holders of institutional power are ever focused on the heart of one kid the way a teacher can be.

Principles Make Our Instruction More Coherent and Intentional

Even when we're feeling strong and grounded in our practice, paying explicit attention to the principles that we teach from and within is a useful and sustaining practice. Principles offer a set of intentional, powerful lenses through which to view and reflect on our own practice as teachers. And the benefits of reflection are by now well known, helping teachers to gain deeper critical insight into their own practice (Boud, 2001; Boud et al., 1985; Gay & Kirkland, 2003).

Our principles don't benefit only us, however. They also help us to make our instruction more coherent and purposeful for our students. Research shows that when lessons are more coherently focused around clear goals and principles, students learn more (Erickson, 2002; Guthrie et al., 2000; Seidel et al., 2005). And it makes sense, doesn't it, that when activities are connected to clear purposes, and fit together with other activities and their purposes over time, students can better make use of them for learning.

When I think about coherence, I always think about two classrooms in a study I was involved with (Whitney et al., 2008). Both teachers were working with similar kinds of kids in similar schools, and both teachers were using the same district-provided materials, in this case a set of reading and writing lessons centered on Amelia Earhart. The basic activities and sequence of instruction were the same for these two teachers—activities to support invention, planning, drafting, and revision—and both of them were very good at working with students through these activities. However, one teacher often stepped back to place the activities within a bigger picture. She articulated why a particular strategy was good to use, beyond that assignment. She always made ties between what was happening now and what might happen in the future or in other writing situations, when the same moves would be called for. She even engaged the students in thinking together about why Amelia Earhart was someone worth learning about. The nuts and bolts of this teacher's instruction were basically identical to that of the other teacher, but the framing was clear and coherent. Activities had a place in a broader set of ideas that drove her teaching and that also powered the students' engagement in what they had been asked to do. And when the students wrote, they had a clear sense of why they were doing so: beyond the fact that a teacher had asked them to write, they had things they wanted to say about Amelia Earhart and a sense of who they might say those things to.

This is the power of principles. Principles tie instructional moves together into bigger frames. Principles give activities a "why." Principles offer both teachers and students a way to hook into a bigger picture that unifies and gives significance to what we are doing.

Principles Make Our Practice Shareable

What's more, keying our teaching practice to specific principles makes it share-able. Maybe having your ninth graders write and produce video PSAs about water quality, for example, is local to your specific teaching context, where water quality is a pressing issue and where PSAs are specifically called for in a district curriculum document. So the details of that specific teaching sequence in and of themselves may not be directly useful to a colleague who teaches, say, fiction writing in grade 11 in a distant location. However, the details of that specific teaching practice become *very* useful (and provocative!) to that teacher when they're offered not as an account of one particular assignment but as an example of working with students as they write for authentic audiences according to their different purposes. Perhaps one teacher is having students craft PSAs for an audience of local citizens, and another is having students craft informational books about middle school for rising sixth graders currently attending elementary school—these specifics come together and become mutually informing when they are linked by a shared principle, in this case "Writing grows out of many purposes."

Clearly identified principles are the language—and result—of a lively, ongoing conversation among teachers of writing. The principles featured in this book aren't one teacher's intuition or one colleague's version of "what works"; they reflect years of experimentation and collaboration by teachers and of more systematic research and scholarship by both classroom teachers and other educators. In other words, naming and claiming these principles connects us to a long tradition of other teachers of writing who have struggled together to understand the very things we are contending with, and also to whose discussion we ourselves might have something to add.

Take the National Council of Teachers of English (NCTE), for example, whose press is publishing this book and whose members crafted the statement of principles upon which this book is focused. NCTE was founded in 1911, and it was in that first meeting that the *English Journal* (first published in 1912) also was founded. From its beginning, this community of teachers has gathered to talk about issues literacy teachers face—and has made the effort to share thinking via publications, in-person meetings, and, later, online resources and interactions. Each of these texts or events does not stand alone; taken together, they represent a conversation. Through that conversation, some core principles have emerged.

The conversation wouldn't be much of a conversation if people just asserted their own ideas without learning and linking to the ideas of those who have come before. Think about how you talk at a party. You don't walk into a crowded room, take off your coat, clear your throat, and begin immediately to give a speech. No, you take as a given that people who are already there are already talking about interesting things. So you hang up your coat, maybe greet a few people you know, and edge up to a group whose conversation is in midstream. You get a sense of what they are saying, catch up on the thread of talk, before you jump in to add your own ideas. And when you add those ideas, you have some expectation that they'll be listened to and responded to. Others will build off of what you say, maybe to disagree or maybe to add on or explore an implication of what you said. And by the end of the night, you and the other folks you've been talking with all know a bit more than you did when you came in, or at least can ask some new questions. This is only possible because you talked together, taking turns and threading together various comments with shared themes that served as through-lines for the conversation. Shared principles of professional knowledge are like that—they are through-lines for our shared conversation that allow our wonderings, observations, and insights to be talked about outside just our own heads. The guy who interjects a bunch of non sequiturs at the party isn't participating in the same way.

Principles Provoke Inquiry and Reflection

One of my favorite things about clarifying principles for practice is the way they provoke and focus my questions as I teach. A principle like "Writing is social" leads me to "How can I develop writing partnerships for my students?" And systematic inquiry enriches teaching with new information and insight that we can put directly back into teaching (Cochran-Smith & Lytle, 1999, 2001; Fleischer, 1995; Whitney et al., 2008).

One way principles provoke and support inquiry is by making our questions better. Instead of asking, "Why is this not working?" or "Why is this student not learning?," we can ask, "What processes are students engaging in here, and what resources do they need to succeed?" Or "How can I better support this student?" Without thoughtful questions, it's easy to fall into the trap of deficit perspectives that harm students and stop us from doing our best work.

Professional Knowledge for the Teaching of Writing: About the Principles Document

This book, of course, isn't about just any principles; it is grounded in the set of principles laid out in the position statement *Professional Knowledge for the Teaching of Writing*, adopted by NCTE in 2016 and reprinted in the front matter of this book. So let me share a bit of the history behind that document and its meaning as a statement of shared grounding principles for practice, developed, assembled, vetted, and articulated by the professional community of which you as readers, I as author and editor, and the teachers who contributed later chapters are all members.

The history of the Principles, as I'll call them throughout this book, is really two histories: one, the history of the document, and the other, the history of the ideas in it. First, a brief history of the document: NCTE has often taken formal positions on a range of issues inside and outside of the classroom, and in 2004 the statement *NCTE Beliefs about the Teaching of Writing* was adopted by the NCTE Executive Committee. The Executive Committee comprises elected members of NCTE representing all its various sections; they are classroom teachers and teacher educators, like you and me. The origin story of the Principles goes like this: In 2002, that group decided to embark on a two-year focus on writing, discerning NCTE's positions on writing and what actions NCTE might choose to take relative to writing. A writing study group was formed, and one product of that group's work was *NCTE Beliefs about the Teaching of Writing* (BATW), which was presented to the leadership of NCTE and approved by its members; the document was ultimately adopted as NCTE's official position on the teaching of writing in November 2004. More than a decade later, the NCTE Executive Committee engaged a wider review and refresh of existing policy statements, updating some and sundowning others. This provided an opportunity to incorporate new research into the statement on writing as well as make it responsive to changing contexts, though the basic ideas in the document remained consistent. A committee was appointed to examine and update BATW, and the product of that group was eventually adopted as *Professional Knowledge for the Teaching of Writing*. While I admire the document, its name is long, and PKFTW is not a very sayable acronym, so in this book, I'll usually call it the Principles.

The history of the ideas that constitute the Principles document is of course much more complex. The next chapter presents a bit of the background and support for each of the ten principles; here, I want to step back a bit to offer a perspective on the community discernment process by which these ideas gain currency, are vetted, and become shared beliefs of a professional community. That process is less formalized than was the creation of the actual Principles document, but it matters nonetheless because it shows that the principles we come to identify as a community aren't just the opinions of a few powerful people, not fads or the educational flavor-of-the month.

We gain professional knowledge from formal and informal inquiry, in and out of the classroom. So some of our shared professional knowledge comes from teachers who develop wonderings from their own daily teaching practice, who systematically investigate those, and who then make changes in practice from what they find as well as share their learning with other teachers. This movement and source of professional knowledge we call teacher research or practitioner research (Cochran-Smith & Lytle, 1992, 2009). Its history is rich, dating to the beginnings of research on writing and having roots in the work of progressive educators like John Dewey and his colleagues in the United States as well as others like Lawrence Stenhouse in the United Kingdom later on. Teacher research as a needed and legitimate source of knowledge for practice grew in influence in the US largely through the National Writing Project (e.g., MacLean & Mohr, 1999), whose teachers-teaching-teachers philosophy fit well with teacher research and whose teacher-leaders rightly perceived that there really was not much empirical information available about what worked for writing instruction in the K–12 classroom from *any* source. Teacher research also took hold in teacher networks and organizations serving teachers such as the Bread Loaf School of English (whose DeWitt Wallace-Reader's Digest–funded large-scale network of rural teachers included teacher research as a core component) (Goswami & Stillman, 1987). NCTE and its members have been ever-present through these developments (Fleischer, 1995; Stock, 2001, 2005), and the organization has long supported teacher research, providing venues for its publication through its journals and conferences, hosting countless convention sessions dedicated to supporting teacher research or sharing its results.

Meanwhile, knowledge that confirms, extends, and at times challenges what we can learn directly from practice also comes from qualitative and quantitative studies originating outside the classroom (but almost always carried out with insight from teacher partners). This work is usually led by university faculty. These researchers are NCTE members too. NCTE as an organization has supported this kind of knowledge generation for the teaching of writing through its research-focused journals such as *Research in the Teaching of English* and *English Education*, through the NCTE Research Foundation, and through other research supports such as the CEE (now ELATE) Research Initiative. It also encourages and recognizes this strand of research through mentorship and dissemination structures such as the L. Ramon Veal Research Seminar and the Research Strand at the NCTE Annual Convention, in which proposals go through a research-specific peer review process before approval for the Convention Program.

All of this is to say that the knowledge expressed in the Principles is *our* knowledge. It is not just someone's opinion, and it's not just the practice of another teacher. It isn't new or fashionable. It has been vetted by our community, not only in the process of the formal drafting of the Principles document but also, and more important (and much more extensively!), through the vetting and peer review that goes into research collaborations, peer review, reviewing for publications, and putting one's ideas out in front of a conference or roundtable. These are not the ideas of faraway experts, and they are not ideas picked up outside and imposed on our teaching by policymakers from outside. They are *our* ideas.

This means that *Professional Knowledge for the Teaching of Writing* gives us at least these four gifts: It gives us a source of ideas for practice when we need ideas. It gives us a reflective filter for enhancing and deepening the practices we already work with. It gives us an evaluative filter for evaluating practice suggested (or mandated) by others. And it gives us a place to stand in the face of bad ideas for practice or when we need to defend practices we know are good for student writers.

In This Book

The rest of this book offers a chance to think through this powerful set of principles so that you can make use of them. It is a chance not only to consider principles on the abstract level, but also to see and hear from other teachers exactly what these ideas look like in real writing classrooms with real kids. Along the way, side boxes invite you to reflect and think further about applications to your own teaching every day.

In Chapter 2, I unpack each of the ten principles laid out in *Professional Knowledge for the Teaching of Writing*. Chapters 3–9 are invited contributions from teachers of high school writers who have spent some time thinking about what these principles look like in their own practice and have described those so that we can think together about them. Chapter 10 backs up again to a bigger picture, adding all of this up into a discussion of professional knowledge and how we grow it, helping you form a clear plan going forward. I close with an annotated bibliography, written—not in academic prose, but in teacher-friendly language—to encourage you to keep exploring, questioning, and reconsidering as you continue this conversation.

A Vision of Writing and Writing Instruction

Chapter
Two

A Vision of Writing and Writing Instruction

For too many years, teaching writing mostly meant teaching handwriting. Or it meant having students copy pieces of writing, the idea being that by doing so, one would internalize the genius of the authors of excellent texts. And while that seems like a long time ago, much more recently and in many classrooms right now, teaching writing actually just means *assigning* writing. That is, writing prompts are developed and handed to students to complete, and then when the students have done some writing, those pieces of writing are collected and evaluated. In that scenario, teachers assign and evaluate, and students write, but where is the actual *teaching* of writing?

Applebee and Langer (2009, 2011) found that in secondary classrooms, the truth is that very little writing happens at all: in a week, a typical student writes about 1.6 pages in English class and another 2.1 in math, social studies, and science combined. More strikingly, of all the writing that students are asked to do, only 19 percent of assignments call for writing a paragraph or more; most student writing in school is short answers of a sentence or less (Applebee &

Langer, 2011, p. 15). What does happen can be characterized as *receptive* more than it is *productive*: students copy things down, take notes as a teacher talks, or answer questions posed by a teacher or on a handout. Only occasionally is this stream of activity interrupted by actually composing texts in which there are decisions to be made by the writer. Rarer still are opportunities to revise, or to write for an audience other than the teacher.

This reality stands in contrast to what we know from large-scale studies of writing and from our own experience with teaching young writers to be effective: writers need things like volume (that is, time spent writing), feedback, support for engaging in writing processes, and well-chosen strategy instruction (Graham & Perin, 2007; Graham & Sandmel, 2011; Hillocks, 1984). What's more, they need environments for learning to write that offer authenticity, support, and safety to take risks; without these, students often will choose not to write at all. After all, how can one learn to do something one never practices? And what's more, how can one get good at something one doesn't care about?

Further, policies or curriculum materials we encounter often take explicit or implicit positions at odds with what this research has shown to be true. For example, more than fifty years of research make a strong case against decontextualized grammar instruction, showing instead that teaching grammar within authentic writing experiences is most effective (Weaver, 1996; Weaver et al., 2006). Yet many of us find ourselves assigned to teach stand-alone courses entitled "Grammar and Mechanics," or work in districts where, since the state tests include multiple-choice grammar questions, teachers are expected to have students practicing with multiple-choice grammar questions. What are teachers to do in situations like that? Being able to articulate a clear principle, a principle that is named and supported by a respected professional organization and backed by research, helps us navigate and even advocate.

Many of these principles are well known enough to be a kind of common knowledge among teachers, but their familiarity can sometimes mean that we take them for granted. What were once powerful and practical ideas can sometimes become meaningful yet somewhat abstract ideals—especially in a world of increasingly decontextualized testing and mandated curricula that arise from that testing—and these in turn can inadvertently fade into the background as our attention is drawn to urgent practicalities rather than the core ideas that underlie them. Our practice drifts off course from what we had charted. We look up one day and find that despite what we say we value, we have become less than the teachers we meant and want to be. Sometimes this happens because we reach for what's expedient, not realizing how it might change the course of our practice. Other times, someone hands us materials to use, not trusting our judgment or perhaps even hoping to accomplish a separate agenda despite us.

In the rest of this chapter, I take a closer look at each of the principles. You'll see the way the principle has been articulated by our NCTE colleagues, and I also highlight some points to notice about each one. I also offer some ideas for further reading about each of the principles. But first, let's stop for a moment to think about this idea of "professional knowledge" a little more carefully. As teachers, we often find people wanting to impart knowledge to us, or critical of knowledge they feel we lack. What do our NCTE colleagues mean when they talk about "professional knowledge?"

What Professional Knowledge Is and Isn't

Many people involved in education seem to perceive professional knowledge as something teachers receive and then have. That is, the vision of knowledge is like a package, and the vision of learning by teachers is like passing the package from one owner to another. Instead, the vision of professional knowledge for the teaching of writing articulated in the NCTE document *Professional Knowledge for the Teaching of Writing*—and developed in this book—is a dynamic vision that means constant learning, constant reflection, and constant interrogation. It's a vision of knowledge as something that we make, that grows over time. The set of contrasts in Table 2.1 makes the point.

It's a mistake to think about professional knowledge for teaching writing as simply knowing about writing; teaching writing involves specialized teaching knowledge going beyond writing itself. Nor is it enough to think about professional knowledge for teaching writing as simply knowing how to "deliver" one curriculum, as seems to be the assumption behind much recent policy and ensuing

Table 2.1. About the Principles in *Professional Knowledge for the Teaching of Writing*

They *aren't*...	They *are*. . .
received	made
static	growing
made in the past	alive and in-the-making
authored by others	teachers' own
neutral	political or value-laden
abstract and distant from the classroom	actively engaged in any teaching moment
a total guide to what to do	a set of ideas to discern with
all about skills and achievement	linked to love and how we live in relationships with students and colleagues

"training" activities for teachers. (I won't call these professional development; I see professional development as something much broader, involving development over time of deep understandings in a person who has autonomy to make decisions and implement change as that person sees fit.)

Professional knowledge for teaching writing, then, is not a set of facts or a set of skills; it is a set of understandings about what writing is and what writers need, as well as how we can best support those needs as writers grow. This knowledge can be understood as a set of principles, ideas grounded in research and consistent with experience in practice. This book is about showing what principles such as these really look like in our day-to-day teaching of writing. Let's turn now to each of the principles laid out in *Professional Knowledge for the Teaching of Writing* (and remember that the Principles themselves are printed in the front matter of your book for your convenience; all page number references map to this book).

Writing Grows Out of Many Purposes

Ask any high school student—or even any adult who's been to high school at some point in their life—what high school writing is, and they'll most likely say it's writing essays for a teacher. In that scenario, the genre is decided for you (essay), the audience is decided for you (the teacher), and most important, the purpose has been decided for you. But what is that purpose? Sadly, in too many cases, the purpose of having that high school student write that essay is either to demonstrate that they've read something, or to demonstrate that they know how to write an essay. That is, many times, school writing is purposeless beyond the fact that it is school writing.

Now think, in contrast, of how writing most often goes in your normal life as an adult. I can't think of a time when, as an adult, I have set out to write something simply to prove that I could do so. No, I write because I find I have something to say. There's a wedding and I am to give a toast, and it's important to me to express to the bride what she has meant to me. Or there has been a troubling incident on the playground at my child's school, and so I need to write an email to his teacher reporting what my son has told me about it. Or there's an issue of some concern at work, and I'm writing to my department head to make my position clear. Or I want money, and so I am writing a grant asking someone to give me that money. In all of these cases, writing comes purpose-first. Rather than choosing a genre and a deadline, and then thinking of a topic and imagining a reason for writing about that topic, real writers in real life *begin* from purposes. These purposes are communicative needs, relationship needs, tasks we want to accomplish. And all of our decisions about the form of the writing and our process of creating the writing tend to follow from that.

For us as teachers of writing, this means that we need to do two things. First we need to consider what students' authentic purposes for writing might actually be. What do they care about? What are their communicative needs? What are the tasks they wish to accomplish in your classroom, in the school, in their lives, in the world? What do they have to say?

Of course, once we consider what students' purposes for writing might be, we won't get very far if we don't take those purposes seriously. I think this is the reason why school writing has often remained so inauthentic. If you have students writing about what they care about, it means that you care about it too. It means that you see students' own purposes as worthy of classroom attention. Schools have not always valued students' purposes for anything. The purpose of the student, according to one vision of school, is simply to *be molded* in the way that the school intends. So already, by attending to students' own purposes for writing, we are taking the stand that students have things to say, that those things can be important, and that one aim of school is to help students accomplish their own purposes, rather than solely accomplishing purposes that someone else has set for them.

The second thing that we have to do, if we value the principle of professional knowledge that *writing grows out of many purposes*, is to actually engage students in writing for *many* purposes. That is, the "many" matters. Think about a year in the life of a writer in your class. What are the different reasons your students write during the course of a year? Because they are in school, it is appropriate that at times—relatively rare times, one hopes—they will write for the purpose of proving they read something. Or they will write for the purpose of demonstrating achievement of some writing skill, as on a test. But for what other purposes have they written? To inform a reader of something? To persuade a reader of something? What about to explore their own thinking on a topic, as in exploratory journal writing, quick-writing, writing before a discussion, or writing informal notes in a reader's notebook or writer's notebook? Have they written to express emotion? Have they written to effect change in the world in some concrete way, such as influencing a policy or acquiring resources they need?

For further reading:

Fleischer, C., & Andrew-Vaughan, S. (2009). *Writing outside your comfort zone: Helping students navigate unfamiliar genres*. Heinemann.

Fletcher, R. (2013). *What a writer needs* (2nd ed.). Heinemann.

Newkirk, T., & Kittle, P. (Eds.). (2013). *Children want to write: Donald Graves and the revolution in children's writing*. Heinemann.

Sipe, R. B., & Rosewarne, T. (2006). *Purposeful writing: Genre study in the secondary writing workshop*. Heinemann.

Writing Is Embedded in Complex Social Relationships and Their Appropriate Languages

When we say that writing is embedded in complex social relationships and their appropriate languages, part of what we mean is simply that how we write depends on contexts, purposes, and audiences in ways that are complex and dynamic. As relationships change, as power and privilege are distributed and withheld, as our reasons for reading and for writing evolve and influence one another, as cultural contexts amplify some voices and drown out others, as communities form around and are transformed by texts—all of these movements influence what is written and how.

To offer a basic example, I use different language in a letter to my mother than in a letter to my son, than in a letter to the editor for my local paper. They're all letters, so they do have some features in common, such as a salutation at the beginning. But they'll sound quite different from one another, won't they? Part of this difference is because of audience; for example, my son is six years old and has a different vocabulary from that of my mom, who is significantly older than six. Writing to a specific reader, I calibrate the register I use—that is, the tone, formality, and complexity of the language—to that specific reader's understanding.

But the ways writing changes as you move from context to context is more than simply identifying register. It's not just degree of formality, and it's not just vocabulary, or the complexity of the sentences I use to match some notion of my reader's "reading level." Instead, it's more about my relationships to readers and to the material that I'm writing about. First, let's think about my relationships with readers. Those letters to my son and to my mom are written within the family context, but that context is complicated. The histories between my mom and me and even between my son and me are different from one another. We have different shared background. We remember some of the same things, but even those things we both remember, we remember differently. A letter that I write to my mom is written in the context of all of the communications we've had before, and the ups and downs of our relationship over the forty-seven years that I've been her daughter. The letter to my son is composed not only with mindfulness of his needs as a reader (such as vocabulary or sentence complexity), but also in the context of my love for him, an all-encompassing love. It's composed in the context of any frustration I might be having with him that day. Maybe he wouldn't put his shoes on when it was time to go out to the bus. Or maybe I'm worried for him because of something that is happening in his life at school. When I'm writing to my son, my writing is imbued with all of my hopes and dreams for him and with my fears about my ability to raise him the way he deserves.

How different these letters are from a letter to the editor of the newspaper. On the one hand, readers of this letter will be strangers to me. Yet as readers of my local paper, they're members of my local community, and we have a shared stake in things that happen here. I have to think about the background knowledge they would have, and also about things that one or the other of us might assume are shared but are actually different. My community includes people of diverse ages, races, ethnic backgrounds, nationalities, income levels, levels of education, desires, sets of experiences. All of those nuances of readers' relationships to me are invoked as I write and as readers read.

This principle of writing as embedded in language and relationships also reveals how power is always inherent in writing, and consequently in writing instruction. Power is inherent in all communication, and language and power are inextricably linked. Students bring rich resources of home language and literacies; however, too often, school has rejected and suppressed these. Students' languages, whether languages other than English or varieties of English, matter. When we position "Standard" English—and a white, academic English at that—as "correct" and other language repertoires of students as "wrong," we further oppression. NCTE has long advocated for more attention (and more knowledgeable, responsive, and transformative attention) to these issues. But too often, teachers have been the oppressors in this dynamic rather than supporters and advocates.

Teaching writing in light of all this complexity means helping writers unpack the power dynamics in the writing situations they encounter. It means providing a variety of audiences for students so that they can gain experience making decisions about language, register, and moving among and/or mixing a range of codes. It means making clear what we don't know but that students do know, especially when it comes to cultural and linguistic knowledge that we may not share. And most important in my mind, it means opening up opportunities for writers to speak to power, using their writing for critique, action, and advocacy. Writing instruction should increase students' power in the world, not diminish it.

For further reading:

Baker-Bell, A. (2020). *Linguistic justice: Black language, literacy, identity, and pedagogy*. Routledge & NCTE.

Baker-Bell, A., Butler, T., & Johnson, L. (2017). The pain and the wounds: A call for critical race English education in the wake of racial violence. *English Education, 49*(2), 116–29.

Baker-Bell, A., Stanbrough, R. J., & Everett, S. (2017). The stories they tell: Mainstream media, pedagogies of healing, and critical media literacy. *English Education, 49*(2), 130–52.

Delpit, L., & Dowdy, J. K. (Eds.). (2008). *The skin that we speak: Thoughts on language and culture in the classroom* (New ed.). The New Press.

Perryman-Clark, S. M. (2012). Toward a pedagogy of linguistic diversity: Understanding African American linguistic practices and programmatic learning goals. *Teaching English in the Two Year College*, *39*(3), 230–46.

Perryman-Clark, S., Kirkland, D. E., & Jackson, A. (2015). *Students' right to their own language: A critical sourcebook*. Routledge.

Smitherman, G. (2000). *Talkin that talk: Language, culture, and education in African America*. Routledge.

Composing Occurs in Different Modalities and Technologies

When you come to think of writing as *composing texts*, you leave space for a wonderful flexibility in the modes in which those texts might be composed and eventually read. I think of a group of students who recently had been working through a unit on "Cultural Identities" in which they had read all kinds of texts that engaged cultures in some way. They read novels, memoirs, and biographies, both graphic and not, in print and in film, texts that focused on people crossing cultures, migrating, making cross-cultural relationships, and so on. Along the way, students composed in an even broader range of modalities: they journaled, created artwork, drew graphs, wrote argumentative essays, drafted fictional para-narratives, sketchnoted, composed and delivered speeches, and more. This rich variety in modes of composition reflects the core of this principle: writing is more than putting words on paper, though it certainly includes that.

Yet so often in schools, I see any composing other than print essays positioned as "just for fun" after the more serious work of essay writing is done. Or I see modes listed on a kind of menu, and kids are to pick one and use it. But think of the texts we encounter outside of school. This morning I read an article in a print periodical. It had photographs with captions alongside it, as well as a graph. Later, I came across a blog post on a related topic; it linked to an archived Twitter chat and a few more blog posts, one of which was in the form of a comic. All of these texts centered on a single theme; all of them moved among modes within a single text.

My focus here isn't on the texts we read alone; behind the texts we read are the composing processes we engage, and it's those processes that move across modalities and platforms in the language of this principle. Multimodal composition isn't just about being able to compose more than one way; it's also about deciding among modes at a particular moment in time, shaping texts that integrate multiple modes, and combining or mixing modes in ways that make ideas more comprehensible or that refresh or transform ideas. Even composing this relatively monomodal, print-based chapter, I engaged sketchnotes on paper, listing in a notebook, voice-to-text composing, moving between document and outline views in a Google Doc, and envisioning the format of the text boxes and side boxes you see on these pages. It's on us to see that students have similar flexibility and support to compose across multiple modes and engage a variety of platforms and tools as they do so.

This means that we need to offer students choices about the platforms and media in which they will compose. Moreover, we need to help them think through the decisions: writers don't just pick media and genres because they sound fun to use; they choose strategically based on the whole context for what they are doing. For example, one colleague has her class brainstorm all the kinds of texts they have encountered around a single theme, then use that as a bank of ideas for their own compositions. Their studies of civil rights and protest movements, for instance, have involved reading a range of texts, including feature films, YouTube videos, informational articles, web archives, museum catalogs, print and graphic memoirs, a novel, protest songs, and more. They have received instruction via print, one-on-one conferring with the teacher, small-group work sessions, and a class Flipgrid used for sharing resources and beginning ideas as well as for receiving video feedback from peers. Now they have chosen a specific group, person, or movement to focus on and will create products that teach classmates about those movements in a walk-through exhibit. Incidentally, these products also span multiple modes: one group composes a one-minute video about the late Congressman John Lewis; another makes a comic book about access to birth control; a third group presents a song and slideshow about the Children's March in Birmingham in 1963. These students have composed texts they think they can get their peers to engage with, in a short period of time as they browse a noisy room, in ways that convey the information they feel their audience most needs to learn about.

For further reading:

Ávila, J., & Pandya, J. Z. (Eds.). (2012). *Critical digital literacies as social praxis: Intersections and challenges* (New ed.). Peter Lang.

Hicks, T. (2013). *Crafting digital writing: Composing texts across media and genres*. Heinemann.

Hicks, T. (Ed.). (2015). *Assessing students' digital writing: Protocols for looking closely*. Teachers College Press.

Lankshear, C., & Knobel, M. (2011). *New literacies: Everyday practices and social learning* (3rd ed.). Open University Press.

Mills, K. A., Stornaiuolo, A., Smith, A., & Pandya, J. Z. (Eds.). (2017). *Handbook of writing, literacies, and education in digital cultures* (1st ed.). Routledge.

National Writing Project, DeVoss, D. N., Eidman-Aadahl, E., & Hicks, T. (2010). *Because digital writing matters: Improving student writing in online and multimedia environments*. Jossey-Bass.

Conventions of Finished and Edited Texts Are an Important Dimension of the Relationship between Writers and Readers

As I mentioned earlier, if you're like me, you frequently have the experience of being at a party or some other group setting in which someone finds out that you teach English and then immediately launches into sharing their opinions about grammar and language conventions. This can take a couple of different forms, including:

- "Why don't they teach grammar anymore?"
- "My teacher had us diagramming sentences. I loved doing that!"
- "The teachers should count off five points for every mistake."
- "You wouldn't believe the grammar of people who apply for jobs at my company. Schools have gone downhill!"

I always hear in these conversations a kind of judgment of me and my work today. An accusation: You don't teach grammar the way you should! Or, You're doing a bad job because someone made an error in a piece of writing in my office!

It's true, I would like it if all of the writers I have taught could produce error-free documents when it mattered to do so. This is in fact a goal of writing instruction; however, it's not the *only* goal. And that's where things get tricky for us in making decisions about how to teach writing day to day.

Of course conventions matter. When students apply for jobs, or submit grant proposals, or even write for tests, we want them to have produced clean, error-free text. We want this for students because we don't want anything to get in the way of their messages being heard by readers. And we also don't want anything to stand in the way of their success in life, where people will sometimes evaluate their intelligence or their preparedness for a given task by the presence or absence of errors in their writing. That's true.

The problem with this truth is that for too long we have stubbornly tried to reach these goals using means that are absolutely ineffective. We have more than fifty years of solid research telling us that isolated grammar exercises do nothing for the writer except, perhaps, make the writing worse by increasing anxiety and by taking class time that could be spent actually writing. And yet it is still common to see stand-alone grammar courses in schools, or to see students doing grammar exercises for homework without any real writing attached. There's a place for the grammar book, and there is even a place for doing exercises, but that place is *right next to doing some actual writing.* That is, it doesn't work to teach me the comma rules until I am trying to write something that requires using commas. When I'm doing that, I have a *need* to know the rules about commas. At that moment, I can step aside briefly, learn some rules through explicit teaching, and even practice using those a bit. But then I need to turn back to my draft and try to make changes in it, and from there continue drafting, revising, and editing with more awareness of where the commas do and don't belong. We know from research that this is truly the only way to improve one's performance of correct English grammar in writing. To effectively teach grammar, we have to do it *in context*.

What's more, we teachers know that these "rules" of written expression are really conventions of groups of human language users, not fixed and immovable truths. As such, they're susceptible to the systems of privilege and power that influence all of us, all the time. It's important to remember, as discussed earlier, how the conventions of written English as typically taught in schools are more accurately the conventions of Standard Written English. And that is NOT the only English that matters. This means for teachers that we must teach not only how to write conventionally, but also where those conventions come from and how they change.

For further reading:

Anderson, J. (2005). *Mechanically inclined: Building grammar, usage, and style into writer's workshop.* Stenhouse.

Baker-Bell, A. (2020). *Linguistic justice: Black language, literacy, identity, and pedagogy.* Routledge & NCTE.

Hyler, J., & Hicks, T. (2017). *From texting to teaching: Grammar instruction in a digital age.* Routledge.

Killgallon, D. (1998). *Sentence composing for high school: A worktext on sentence variety and maturity.* Boynton/Cook.

Kolln, M. (2007). *Rhetorical grammar: Grammatical choices, rhetorical effects.* Pearson Education.

Muhammad, G. (2020). *Cultivating genius: An equity framework for culturally and historically responsive literacy.* Scholastic. [See especially the section on skills.]

Noden, H. R. (2011). *Image grammar: Teaching grammar as part of the writing process* (2nd ed.). Heinemann.

Turner, K. H., Abrams, S. S., Katić, E., & Donovan, M. J. (2014). Demystifying digitalk: The what and why of the language teens use in digital writing. *Journal of Literacy Research, 46*(2), 157–93.

Everyone Has the Capacity to Write; Writing Can Be Taught; and Teachers Can Help Students Become Better Writers

By now you've heard about the differences between a growth mindset and a fixed one for learning in all kinds of areas (Dweck, 2006). A fixed mindset says, "You're either born with this or you're not; you have it or you don't," whereas a growth mindset says, "With effort I can get better." Writing is something at which every person can improve. There are surely individual differences that influence learning to write, but every single writer can get better at doing so over time. When student writers share this mindset, they accept feedback more readily and are more willing to write and revise—things we know are essential if they are to improve. In contrast, when they see writing as a gift that you either have or you don't, they tend to avoid writing altogether (Charney et al., 1995; Palmquist & Young, 1992; Whitney, 2018).Why would you work on something you feel you have no chance of accomplishing?

This principle, at its heart, is a kind of prerequisite for any writing instruction. After all, if writers are already born with whatever talent they're going to have, what is the point of teaching writing to begin with? If writing ability is some kind of magic with which some people have been blessed and others have not, then why have a writing class? Simply have the gifted writers do all the writing in our society and spend your instructional time and energy on things you can actually influence! It seems fundamental to being a teacher to assume that a thing can be taught.

However, many of us have not always expressed this belief in our actions as teachers of writing. For many of us, most of our energy around writing instruction involves designing excellent assignments, or preparing clear and explicit directions for students to follow in a prompt, or creating detailed rubrics with which to assess written products. All of these can be valuable parts of the work of teaching writing, but none of them is actually instructing a writer in how to do something that writers need to do. Many participants in the National Writing Project describe a transition through their experiences in that network, from simply assigning writing to teaching writing (Whitney & Friedrich, 2013). That is, they realized over time that they had been assigning writing to students at the beginning and assessing the performance of those students at the end, but they hadn't been doing much along the way to support students in learning as they worked through writing tasks. Once they had adopted a mindset that every student can be a writer and that with instruction any writer can improve, the teachers then found themselves wanting to support writers along the way in much more direct and engaged ways.

Teaching writing rather than simply assigning writing means working while students are writing to discern what they are struggling with and teaching what they need at that moment to work through the struggle. It means making sure writers get feedback (from you, from peers, or from other adults) before a piece is finished, not only when it's too late to make changes. It means checking in through conferring, asking students to report on their processes along the way, or having students look back at past writing experiences to identify strategies they might find helpful now.

It also means finding ways to believe in and invest in what writers are doing. I had a teaching friend who used to say that his best skill for teaching high school writing was that he was "easily impressed." He was joking, but there was some truth in his comment as well: adolescent writers are indeed impressive. They are trying new things, putting their work in front of us when it's risky, at a time in their lives when everything is changing and their place in the world does not feel secure. And when my friend said he was easily impressed, he meant that he was able to enthuse about student writers' early attempts. He could get excited about what a writer was trying to do, finding something to love about each draft, and his expression of that love and excitement made the critical feedback he also had to give much more palatable. He communicates such hope for what the writer is working on that students then strive to live up to that. Doesn't every writer need this kind of faith and encouragement from a loving—even if critical—mentor? How can you find something to love about every piece of writing you work with?

For further reading:

Applebee, A. N., & Langer, J. A. (2013). *Writing instruction that works: Proven methods for middle and high school classrooms.* Teachers College Press.

Bomer, K. (2010). *Hidden gems: Naming and teaching from the brilliance in every student's writing.* Heinemann.

Fu, D., & Shelton, N. R. (2007). Including students with special needs in a writing workshop. *Language Arts, 84*(4), 325–36.

Kittle, P. (2008). *Write beside them: Risk, voice, and clarity in high school writing.* Heinemann.

National Writing Project, & Nagin, C. (2006). *Because writing matters: Improving student writing in our schools* (Rev. & upd. ed.). Jossey-Bass.

Olson, C. B. (2011). *The reading/writing connection: Strategies for teaching and learning in the secondary classroom* (3rd ed.). Pearson.

Writing Is a Process

Beginning in the 1960s and extending through the 1970s and 1980s, a revolution occurred in the study and teaching of writing. This revolution, incited by pioneers of writing research such as James Britton and Nancy Martin in the UK and Janet Emig, Donald Graves, Don Murray, and Peter Elbow in the US, centered on a key innovation in approaching writing: to understand writing, it was important to look not only at finished written texts but also at the things writers did to make those texts. That is, writing is a process, not only a product, and to understand and improve how people learn to write, it behooves us to look at that process.

This notion, now a commonplace, spread rapidly in the 1970s and 1980s, in large part through the concurrent and related growth of the National Writing Project (NWP). The National Writing Project, now a national network of local sites engaging teachers in writing and professional development, began in 1974 with a single roomful of teachers sharing and analyzing their own effective classroom practices, as well as reading what little published research was then available on how people learn to write (Sublette, 1973). But most of all, they *wrote*—and the practice of spending time writing daily, doing all kinds of writing from journaling to crafting fiction, poetry, memoir, and/or professional writing, has continued as a core feature of the NWP experience (Blau, 1993; Lieberman & Wood, 2001; Whitney & Friedrich, 2013). By writing themselves, teachers rediscover the processes in which writers (now including themselves!) must engage when approaching a writing invitation or prompt, when inventing, planning, drafting, seeking and receiving feedback, revising, editing, publishing, and so on. This in turn both connects them empathetically to students as fellow writers and puts them in a position to provide support for students along the way.

In many places, the idea of "writing process" is now such a commonplace as to have lost some of its revolutionary meaning. I remember applying for a high school teaching job, the second one I held. Around the interview table, the English department chair asked me the question, "How would you describe the writing process?" Coming fresh from a summer spent writing and learning with the National Writing Project, I launched into an excited discussion about the many ways writers work, the recursive rounds of drafting, feedback, and revision that many texts receive, and the needs of writers as they varied with audience and purpose. "That's nice," the chair commented dryly, "but here, we do prewriting, drafting, revising, editing, and publishing." Oh. Okay.

But reducing the notion of "writing process" to a set of steps that teachers must push students through does a disservice to students and to the complexity that truly is in any one writing process. Writers engage in processes. Writing instruction, it follows, must involve opportunities to engage in those processes with support. And while there are some who say we are in a "postprocess" era or who see a process orientation as somehow disconnected from learning writing skills, the truth is that a process orientation gives us the best chance of actually getting to know our students as writers well enough to teach them (Whitney & Johnson, 2017). As individuals struggle with different things, it takes flexibility to help writers find ways of working through those struggles. That, of course, is a process.

In our classrooms, this means dedicating time in class to actually engaging in writing, not just bringing in writing that has been done elsewhere. It means attending to the ways pieces of writing develop—in stages that are not always predictable, with starts and stops, sometimes changing direction along the way.

It means offering opportunities for revision, knowing that only rarely is our first attempt good enough to meet its purpose. And it means engaging in writing of our own, both in front of the students and in our lives outside the classroom. When we write in front of students, they see how we too are unsure how to begin or end, how we too make changes along the way, even deleting hard-won text when we see it isn't working as we wish. And by writing in our lives both within and beyond the classroom, we also find ourselves "in the thick of it" in ways that make us better able to see what problems students are likely to be having as well. We can approach students writer to writer and suggest strategies that have sometimes worked for us. The value of this cannot be understated; after all, would you take skiing lessons from an instructor who never even put on their skis?

For further reading:

Atwell, N. (1998). *In the middle: New understandings about writing, reading, and learning* (2nd ed.). Boynton/Cook.

Kittle, P. (2008). *Write beside them: Risk, voice, and clarity in high school writing*. Heinemann.

Pritchard, R. J., & Honeycutt, R. L. (2007). Best practices in implementing a process approach to teaching writing. In S. Graham, C. A. MacArthur, & J. Fitzgerald (Eds.), *Best practices in writing instruction* (pp. 28–49). Guilford Press.

Whitney, A. E., & Johnson, L. L. (2017). Speaking Truth to Power: The persistent relevance of a writing process orientation. *English Journal, 106*(4), 82–85.

Writing Is a Tool for Thinking

There's a pervasive popular belief about writing that goes like this: First, you think the thoughts. Then you write those thoughts down. The writing, this story goes, is a kind of transcription that you do after all of the thinking is done.

However, any of us who has tried to write something can attest that this isn't quite the case. Even when you think you have all of the ideas mapped out, new ideas occur as you're writing, or some of the ideas you thought you would use turn out to be not too relevant, or the arrangement you thought would be best fails as you try to construct it—until, faced with the problem *while writing*, you come up with something different. Writing is not only a way of noting one's thinking; it is a way of thinking.

So far in my day today, I've used writing for thinking a number of times. When I woke up this morning, I did a quick gratitude practice in my notebook. Doing the writing helps me to *recall* the things that I could be grateful for; when I crawled out of bed too early, being grateful for anything was far from my mind.

And the practice as a whole actually works to *change my mindset* and approach to the day. While I'm likely to remember my gratitudes without writing them down, writing them actually *changes the feelings* that I feel, from grouchy to grateful. Not long after that, I made a quick to-do list, as I had much I wanted to accomplish this morning. Drafting this chapter was one of them, but so was stopping by my daughter's school to drop off a form, tidying up the top of the pantry before I lose my mind (piles of mail are literally sliding off of the cabinet as we walk past), responding to a draft one of my students had sent, replying to a few emails that can't really wait until Monday, and taking some chicken out of the freezer to thaw for dinner. My to-do list helped me think. In writing it, I automatically started *planning* when I would do each task and what would be involved. What's more, now that I've written them down, I have *freed up* some of my memory so that I can think in a conscious way about other things and let the unconscious work of remembering these items go.

Then, of course, I started working on this chapter. I had a list of points I knew I wanted to make, but as I've been writing them, I've been able to *revise* and *refine* several of those points. At one moment during my writing session this morning, I became so confused about what to do that I switched over to my email and composed a note to the editor of this book. Of course, that email is going to help me materially, in that she will reply, and her reply will include direct answers to some of my questions. However, it's also the case that just by composing the email, I was able to answer a few of my questions for myself. In fact, about half of the original email I wrote, I ended up deleting before sending because, having written it, I had *resolved my confusion* and no longer needed her input. Writing can do this. Later today, I'll head to a Google Doc where a friend and I have agreed to *generate ideas* for a future book project. We aren't sure of the focus of the book yet; we have a broad topic but are still exploring. We use writing to do this by adding to our notes each week after using the week to *reflect* and to collect potential resources. The purpose of that Google Doc isn't to express ideas we already have; it's to see those ideas laid out alongside one another and *examine* them, and to build on those ideas to *invent* further ideas that neither of us has had yet.

So writing is a tool for thinking. In my morning alone, I used writing-for-thinking to recall, to change my mind, to change my feelings, to plan, to free up memory, to revise and refine ideas, to resolve confusion, to generate ideas, to reflect, to examine, and to invent. I bet you can add more by reviewing a day or two in your own life as a writer.

For our teaching, this means that we can and should turn to writing all the time, throughout the class period and through a sequence of instruction. Rather than framing writing as a culminating activity, we should present writing as a means of access to any and all material we teach. It also leads many teachers of writing to become official or unofficial ambassadors for writing to learn within their school communities, helping lead colleagues who teach science or history or music away from assigning term papers and correcting grammar toward using notebooks, inviting informal journaling or quick-writing, and more.

For further reading:

Anderson, P., Gonyea, R. M., Anson, C. M., & Paine, C. (2015). The contributions of writing to learning and development: Results from a large-scale multi-institutional study. *Research in the Teaching of English*, *50*(2), 199–235.

Donovan, S. J. (2020). Navigating public and private writing spaces and places: A "room" of my own. *Voices from the Middle*, *28*(1), 10–15.

Emig, J. (1977). Writing as a mode of learning. *College Composition and Communication*, *28*(2), 122–28.

Murphy, S., & Smith, M. A. (2020). *Writing to make an impact: Expanding the vision of writing in the secondary classroom*. Teachers College Press. [See especially Chapter 7, "Writing to Figure Things Out," and Chapter 8, "Writing to Think Critically."]

Writing Has a Complex Relationship to Talk

Last week I was working on drafting another portion of this book when I got stuck. After struggling to start a paragraph, erasing it, trying again, and erasing that version too, I got up to flip the laundry and grab a snack. Then I walked outside to place some mail in the mailbox and bring out the garbage cans. As I walked, without realizing it, I found myself talking. In my talk, I rehearsed various ways of saying what I had struggled to write in the chapter. In fact, I didn't even know I was doing this until a neighbor walked by with her dog, and I realized I was talking to myself—aloud. I went back to the computer and was able to write the troubling passage.

A few days later, my writing group met to discuss a draft of the chapter. They had read it in advance, and via a Zoom video conference we met to share feedback. I asked them to focus specifically on any places they noted that were unclear. They gamely pointed to some places they didn't understand, and in response to their questions, I talked. They listened and took notes. As I spoke, I had some new ideas I hadn't even included in the draft, and I also found words to better express some ideas I had tried to write that were muddy.

Making appropriate use of talk in students' writing processes can be really difficult. For one thing, people usually do need quiet to concentrate on writing, while also needing talk times, and every writer needs both of those things at moments that may conflict. Some teachers designate "quiet corner" or "talk time" spaces in their rooms. Others alternate time periods between silent time for drafting and things like "turn and talk." Beyond this logistical challenge, there's also the idea that in order to move between writing and talk in ways that work well for writers, you need the right people for writers to talk with. A classroom community has to be there. Peers have to know how to give feedback that is actually useful instead of just parroting what they imagine a teacher might say. Writers need people to talk to who can stand in for the audiences for their writing, and they also need people to talk to who can encourage them when the going gets tough.

All this talk can be confounding in other ways also. I remember having a scheduled observation of my classroom by a principal in the first months of a new teaching job. Entering the room a few minutes after the bell, he saw pockets of kids here and there with their desks facing one another, talking about plans for writing, while others faced forward, working individually and doing their best to ignore the boisterous noise around them. Meanwhile, I was kneeling next to a writer, conferring about how he might rethink the opening to an essay. My principal took all of this in. As I rose to invite him to find a seat and to explain a bit about what we were doing, he seemed flustered. "I'll . . . I need to come back when you're teaching," he finally said, and left the room before I could reply. This principal was actually fully supportive of workshop teaching, of student collaboration, of talk, and of the other things he saw that morning—the problem was, he didn't have a framework for what teaching really looked like within it. And I know I'm not alone in having an experience of this kind—even Nancie Atwell tells a similar anecdote in *In the Middle* (1987).

What this means for teaching is that we need to build opportunities for talk into the supports we plan for our student writers. It also means that engaging students in conferences, whether with a teacher or with one another, is a way not only to give writers feedback on their work but also to help writers rehearse and compose. In one study of conferring in a writer's workshop, I saw teachers Deana Washell and Colleen McCracken frequently using a strategy so simple I initially questioned whether it could even be called a strategy. They would approach a writer and ask, "What are you writing?" The writer would then tell about their work in progress: "Oh, it's a fairy story, and the queen fairy is decreeing that all who wish to enter the magic city must first pay a tax, and everyone is really mad about it." Or, "I'm arguing that we need time for band during the school day; right now it's too early in the morning [before school] and we miss out on sleep we need to learn well." Then the teacher asks a powerful question:

"Oh, is that written in your notebook?"

Sure enough, it often wasn't, and the "stuck" writer who had been at a loss for words could now proceed just by writing down what they had related to the teacher. Simply asking writers to talk about what they're trying to do helps them move along.

Honoring writing's complex relationship to talk in our classrooms might mean conferring more, and differently. It might mean having students record themselves speaking or using voice-to-text as part of their composing process. It might mean establishing student writing groups, or engaging groups in discussing content before and during writing. It might even mean having students write collaboratively so they are forced to speak aloud about their decisions as they work.

For further reading:

Anderson, C. (2000). *How's it going? A practical guide to conferring with student writers.* Heinemann.

Bieler, D. (2018). *The power of teacher talk: Promoting equity and retention through student interactions.* Teachers College Press.

Juzwik, M. M., Borsheim-Black, C., Caughlan, S., & Heintz, A. (2013). *Inspiring dialogue: Talking to learn in the English classroom.* Teachers College Press.

McDonald, J. P., Mohr, N., Dichter, A., & McDonald, E. C. (2013). *The power of protocols: An educator's guide to better practice* (3rd ed.). Teachers College Press.

Writing and Reading Are Related

When I was a senior in high school, the English department's practice was to assign a major research paper consuming most of the second semester of Senior English. Keep in mind that I graduated from high school in 1991: this paper was typed on a computer, although a typewriter was still allowed, but the research itself—the planning and the drafting of the paper—was all done by hand. This paper was a literary analysis paper with critical sources cited. So we chose a novel (mine was *Elmer Gantry*), and then we headed to the school library. I know now that these so-called critical sources we were to cite were actually articles appearing in journals, journals filled with literary criticism written by scholars, scholars who were typically professors of English and whose authority to write those articles rested on long years of study. But I didn't know that when I was a senior in high school. Nor was I handed an academic journal to look at as a way to understand the genre. Instead, my classmates and I were directed to sets of brown volumes alongside the wall of the library, long rows of reference books titled *Nineteenth Century Literary Criticism*, *Twentieth Century Literary Criticism*, or *Contemporary Literary Criticism*. (Apparently nobody was crazy enough to try to write this paper on a work composed before the nineteenth century.) These volumes were encyclopedias of literary criticism containing summaries of the criticism that had been done on particular literary works. Quotes from scholarly articles were included, along with near-indecipherable shorthand citations for those quotes. Our job as students was to collect some predetermined number (20?) of these quotes supporting our reading of the literary text. We copied each quote onto a 3" × 5" notecard using a specific format determined by the teacher, without much explanation as to why we were doing so or why the cards should be formatted as directed. We just did it. Then, after all our cards had been collected and graded, we were to write a paper making an argument for a reading of the text and drawing on these critical sources for support. Now, a paper such as this is a real kind of thing. Scholars doing literary criticism write papers in which they offer a reading of a text and refer to criticism done by others, either as support for what they're saying or to take issue with what has been said. But I didn't know any of this. Writing that paper, I had never read a literary critical essay. So I had no example of what it was I was trying to produce. What's more, although the sources I was quoting were also literary critical essays, I did not read one. I just read quotes from them in the trusty *TCLC*.

I know now that my teachers were working very hard on this assignment. It took lots of invention and collaboration on their part to produce appropriate scaffolding for all of us to do this task with any kind of competence, from teaching us the notecard format, to having us practice formatting the cards, to teaching us an essay format, complete with templates for each section of the paper, into which our work could fit. And let me be clear that I also know at least something about why they were assigning this: at that time, in many colleges, literary criticism would indeed be a genre in which I might (and did go on to) write in college, though I'll tell you right now that I completed a degree in English without ever again utilizing *TCLC*. Looking back now, as a writing teacher and scholar who has assigned many papers, I'm struck by how disconnected my production of this paper was from any and all of my reading.

First, I hope I've already pointed out that this project was completely disconnected from any authentic reading of literary criticism. Whatever you may think about the value of writing a literary critical paper in twelfth grade, you can surely imagine how this assignment might have been different had it been preceded by our reading a few critical articles and analyzing them. Instead, the only works of literary criticism I ever read until I was about a junior in college were papers I composed myself. I can assure you that these were not strong examples of the genre! Second, and more to the point, what I wrote can only marginally be said to truly relate to my reading of the text *Elmer Gantry*. Yes, I read *Elmer Gantry*, and I had some thoughts about it, and maybe those thoughts found their way into my paper. But know that writing that paper is not how I read the book; in fact, all of the writing came more than a month after I had finished reading the novel.

And my reading of that novel was a pretty powerful experience: I read *Elmer Gantry*, a Sinclair Lewis novel about a corrupt preacher, as a kid growing up surrounded by a particularly conservative strand of evangelical Christianity, a kid working to develop a life of faith for myself in that environment but also in a family in which no specific religion was practiced. I read that book hungrily: for clues about what religion meant in my community and others, about the differences between faith and religion, and about the trustworthiness (or untrustworthiness) of self-appointed leaders (and perhaps of all adults). That book got me right in the heart. Twenty-eight years later, I remember a lot of what I thought about *Elmer Gantry*, but I don't remember a thing about what I might have said about it in my research paper. The paper wasn't about my experience of *Elmer Gantry*; as far as I knew, it was about assembling quotes.

Reading and writing are connected. We learn what to expect from written texts by reading other such texts. As writers, part of how we envision readers is by drawing on our own reading experiences. However, in school, reading and writing can become separated unnecessarily. Many times, reading is situated within one course and writing within another, down the hall at a different time of day or even in a different school year. But it doesn't have to be this way.

One important way to better draw on the connection between writing and reading is to engage students in genre study. I don't mean announcing, "Now we will write a sonnet" and listing on the board features of that genre; instead, I mean inviting students to examine a set of texts in a genre and derive from their analysis an idea of not only the features of but also the purposes and contexts for writing in a genre. I learned to do this from the work of Fleischer and Andrew-Vaughan (2009), whose "genre challenge" invites writers into an intentional period of genre study, an approach that I now use with my own students, from preservice teachers to adult doctoral students who are learning research genres.

Working with the connections between reading and writing may also mean inviting students to choose different genres from one another, in the same way that you may have them engaging in choice reading. It could mean having read-alouds at the beginning of every class meeting, giving the class a fresh-in-mind, shared textual experience to draw from in that day's writing lessons (not to mention the simple and, for many adolescents, rare joy of being read to by someone who loves reading and loves *them*). It can mean inviting young adult authors into your class, in person or by videoconference, to talk about the decisions behind the texts kids are reading. I often invite teachers to begin simply by making sure that during every class meeting, students both read and write. Even that small step can provoke big change when the norm is separate classes, and ways of thinking, for writing and for reading.

For further reading:

Fitzgerald, J., & Shanahan, T. (2000). Reading and Writing Relations and Their Development. *Educational Psychologist*, *35*(1), 39–50.

Fleischer, C., & Andrew-Vaughan, S. (2009). *Writing outside your comfort zone: Helping students navigate unfamiliar genres.* Heinemann.

Muhammad, G. (2020). *Cultivating genius: An equity framework for culturally and historically responsive literacy.* Scholastic.

Olson, C. B. (2011). *The reading/writing connection: Strategies for teaching and learning in the secondary classroom* (3rd ed.). Pearson.

Assessment of Writing Involves Complex, Informed, Human Judgment

The teacher-candidates I work with at Penn State arrive in my courses with lots of questions about writing assessment. They usually don't say the word *assessment* at first, but their questions sound like this:

"How do I grade writing fairly? It's too subjective."

"How do I know what's an A, what's a B, etc.?"

"How many As, Bs, Cs, etc. should I give?"

These questions used to make me feel angry. There I was, leading a course focused on building a community of writers, encouraging student voices, helping students take risks, encouraging revision, and establishing authentic audiences for student work. And there they were, focusing on As and Bs. "Bean counters!" I would exclaim to myself.

I've come to understand those questions in a different way. First, evaluation and grading are real parts of a teacher's role, for better or for worse, and so I do work with students to consider a wide range of grading practices, from contract grading to student self-evaluation to many points between. But I also now spend a lot of time differentiating between grading, assessment, and feedback. These are not synonyms!

Grading is putting a score on a student's work for the purpose of completing a report card or transcript or some other means of determining the credit a student shall receive for a given task or course. Grading is done by a teacher, from a position of institutional power. Assessment is something different: assessment is making a judgment about the writing. Assessment asks questions like "How effectively does this piece of writing accomplish the writer's goal for it?" or "How well does this piece of writing fit in with conventions for a piece of this type?" And assessment can be done by a teacher but also by the writer themself or another reader. Grading is about the writer in the context of school; writing assessment is about judging the writing in *its* context.

And while both a grade and some other kind of assessment might constitute forms of feedback for a writer, feedback is really much broader. Feedback is information you get from a reader about how the writing is making sense to them. Feedback can be nonjudgmental, reporting on the reader's experience with a text but not assessing its effectiveness or worth. Feedback can happen while writing as well as after writing. And while a writer can function well without assessment, and certainly without grading, it's really hard to grow as a writer without feedback. Even "I liked that" or "Keep going, I want to know what happens next!" can be valuable feedback for a writer.

Now when teacher candidates ask me those questions about As and Bs, I can reply with questions of my own: "What are you trying to accomplish? Do you want to encourage the writer to go on? Let them know about things they might revise? Help them identify their main point(s)? Give them a sense of a potential reader's reaction? Help them find and correct errors? Compare one student's writing to another? Keep track of how much effort they have put in to the task? Get something to write in the gradebook? Compel them to write at all?" Then they're ready to think more carefully about what they might do next.

The notion that writing assessment involves complex and informed human judgment means that we are responsible for advocating against any machine-scored tool as the only measure of how well a student can write or as the basis for any decisions about students. It means that we are responsible for making our assessment practices clear to students. It means that our assessments should connect in logical ways to what we have actually taught student writers to do.

It does not mean, however, that each and every thing a student writes must be assessed. We need to ask ourselves, "Why am I reading this student work right now?" If our purpose is indeed assessment of what has been learned or what further instruction might be needed, then we assess. But if our purpose is that students receive feedback for revision, or that their work be proofread, or that they know they have been heard, we can get them that feedback in other ways. Sometimes peers can do it—but usually not unless we teach those peers to be helpful. Sometimes we will want to do it ourselves—but that doesn't mean we have to spend every night and weekend underneath an oppressive pile of papers to be graded. I know teachers who read a whole-class set of drafts and then provide a page or so of written feedback for the class as a whole. I know teachers who record a brief voice comment for each writer, much faster and much more personal than doing a formal assessment or even writing comments. Assessments must be matched to purposes; so must the nonassessing feedback we give.

For further reading:

Gallagher, C. W., & E. Turley. (2012). *Our better judgment: Teacher leadership for writing assessment*. National Council of Teachers of English.

McGee, P. (2017). *Feedback that moves writers forward: How to escape correcting mode to transform student writing*. Corwin.

National Council of Teachers of English Assessment Task Force. (2020). *Expanding formative assessment for equity and agency* [Position Statement]. National Council of Teachers of English.

Poe, M., Inoue, A. B., & Elliot, N. (Eds.). (2018). *Writing assessment, social justice, and the advancement of opportunity*. The WAC Clearinghouse; University Press of Colorado.

Sackstein, S. (2017). *Peer feedback in the classroom: Empowering students to be the experts*. ASCD.

Smith, M. A., & Swain, S. S. (2016). *Assessing Writing, Teaching Writers: Putting the Analytic Writing Continuum to Work in Your Classroom*. Teachers College Press & National Writing Project.

Wilson, M. (2006). *Rethinking rubrics in writing assessment*. Heinemann.

Taken as one large helping of text, the *Professional Knowledge for the Teaching of Writing* document is a lot to swallow. But if we look at just the list of principles themselves, we get a good, healthy, digestible meal:

1. Writing grows out of many purposes.
2. Writing is embedded in complex social relationships and their appropriate languages.
3. Composing occurs in different modalities and technologies.
4. Conventions of finished and edited texts are an important dimension of the relationship between writers and readers.
5. Everyone has the capacity to write; writing can be taught; and teachers can help students become better writers.
6. Writing is a process.
7. Writing is a tool for thinking.
8. Writing has a complex relationship to talk.
9. Writing and reading are related.
10. Assessment of writing involves complex, informed, human judgment.

These ideas can guide and ground our decisions as teachers of writing. The district proposes to adopt a new program? Let's think about how it coheres with—or conflicts with—these principles. The teacher next door asks to work together on planning some instruction; where to begin? Let's use these principles to set some priorities. Parents are asking why you're doing something that differs from what they remember from their own school days? Here are research-backed principles around which our professional community has consensus.

A teacher friend of mine used to have these words, printed in magic marker three inches high, on the front of his gradebook/planbook: WHY ARE WE DO-ING THIS? He knew, like most teachers do, how easy it is to drift away from our true intentions and goals for instruction and find ourselves doing things for all kinds of less-important reasons: to satisfy a policy, to fill time, to compel behavior. This is not who we wanted to be as teachers of writing. The ideas expressed in the Principles help bring my friend's question, "Why are we doing this?," back into focus.

In the next section of this book, you'll hear from teachers across the United States who are putting these principles into practice. As you read, notice where you see the principles in play, and ask where those principles have led the teacher-author. The ways they do so are varied, as are the many contexts in which we work, but holding them together is one powerful idea: that principled practice, grounded in our accumulated shared professional knowledge, is in the best interest of our student writers.

The teachers who have written for this book are not here because they're the only teachers who work from sound principles as they teach writing, nor because they are perfect. They teach in cities, suburbs, and rural areas; their classrooms are racially homogenous and racially diverse, filled with affluent students and those experiencing poverty. These teacher-authors are varied in gender, race, age, and education. Some I have known for a long time and others I came to know through working together on this book. They have good teaching days and bad ones. They're simply teachers who, like many of you, care deeply about supporting students in learning to write and work from a set of core ideas instilled through their participation in strong professional communities. All have participated in activities of NCTE; many, as you'll see, have involvement in the National Writing Project—no coincidence when you consider how those two organizations have sponsored learning experiences and knowledge-making experiences for teachers of writing throughout their histories.

I asserted at the outset of this chapter that professional knowledge is made, not just acquired, and that principles can help us to grow professional knowledge. By reading this book and engaging with what I have written so far, you have joined with me in a kind of conversation: we, not just you or I, have begun to build something together. In the pages that follow, you'll find further speakers in our shared learning conversation, and further opportunities to grow your own professional knowledge as a teacher of writing in the context of the principles named in *Professional Knowledge for the Teaching of Writing*.

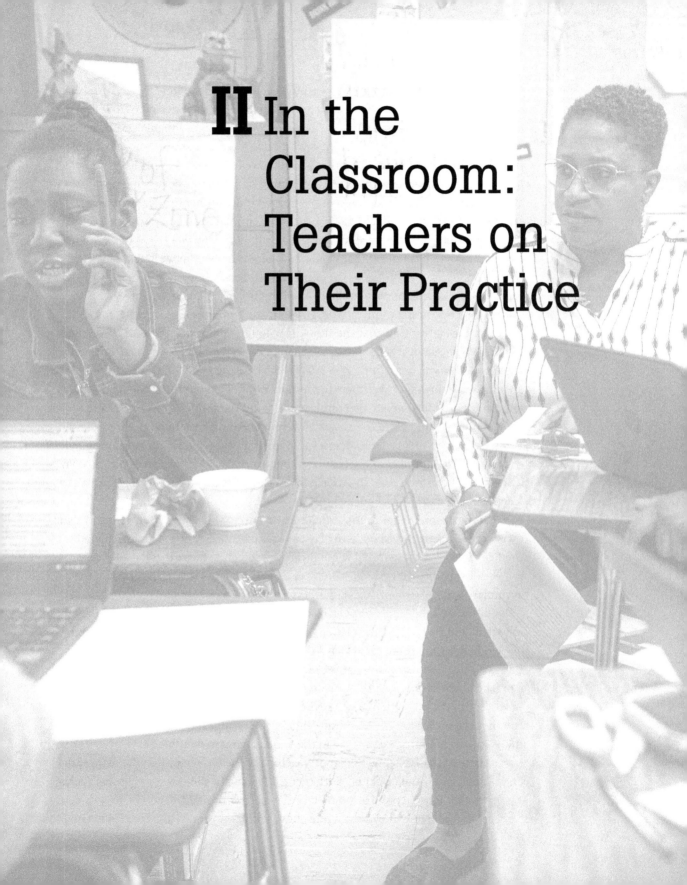

II In the Classroom: Teachers on Their Practice

One thing I've noticed in my own teaching career is that the longer I do this work and the better I get at it, the harder I am to satisfy. I sometimes find myself replaying lessons or discussions that went on in my classroom more than a decade ago, wishing I'd said something different or responded to a student in a more compelling way. Things in my teaching that I could have lived with—even things I worked hard for and was happy with—at the beginning of my career bother me now. I'm always seeing how students could have engaged more authentically, or how an assignment or experience could have been better curated for students. How I could have supported them better along some difficult path. Words I could have said or feedback I could have given that would have better helped my writers along their way. It isn't that I'm getting worse over time—at least I hope not! No, it's that my sense of what is possible as a teacher of writing has expanded over time.

At the beginning of my career, I was satisfied when things were "going well," by which I usually meant that the students willingly did whatever task I asked them to do. Or sometimes it meant that they had done well on an assessment. But now when I think about something going well with student writers, I think not only about getting through it with few bumps and not only about the students producing quality products; now I also think about doing these things in a way that expresses values I hold close to my heart. If, upon reading and thinking through the Principles, I find them sound, doesn't it follow that they should thread through all of my teaching, not just on my best days, but every day? My standards for my own work rise. The more I care about principles, the more I find I want to improve as a teacher and change what I am doing.

In the chapters that follow, you'll hear from teachers as they describe, in their own words, practices in their own classrooms that express the values articulated in the Principles. You'll see what these principles look like for real colleagues dealing with living, breathing kids. You'll see as well students writing, and you'll see exemplary ways of supporting students as they grow as writers.

But what I especially hope you will notice is how these teachers are thinking about and revising their practices over time. None of these teachers is saying, "Look, here's something great that I do" (even though they really are doing great things). They don't stop at what is exemplary: each chapter describes not only a practice but also some of the learning that went into the development of that practice, or how that practice was revised from some earlier way of doing things. In fact, it is these revisions in teaching—thoughtful changes in teaching practice over time—that I find most interesting in the varied chapters that follow.

Many of these chapters begin in teaching *problems*. That is, you'll hear teachers talking about how students' work seemed lacking in some way, or how students were struggling to accomplish some task the teacher thought would be easy. These teachers describe how they respond to these problems in ways that resonate with the Principles our NCTE colleagues have identified. Other times, they describe how they start from strengths students have or interests the students bring with them to the classroom, and the teachers then work to find ways of extending those strengths and interests. What I like best about these chapters, and something I value about the Principles and about the messy, imperfect process of striving to teach in ways that resonate with these principles, is this: teaching from principles places responsibility for success on teachers. That is, when students struggle with something, these teachers don't say, "Well, our kids can't do that." Instead, they say, "What help do the kids need in order to do this better?" The teachers don't say, "Well, first I have to get them through the assessment and *then* I'll be able to teach beyond that"; instead, they say, "What are the most important things I need to get done with these students this year?"

And this: Instead of taking teaching problems personally, feeling like a failure, giving up, or feeling stupid, these teachers get curious. They start wondering. They ask, "How can I learn more about what is needed here?" These teachers are *unsatisfied* in the best possible way. It's a paradox of teaching writing that the better we get at it, the more unsatisfied we become with doing things the same old way year after year and hoping they work. These principles prod us in the direction of professional growth.

Reading Chapters 3–9

One way to approach these chapters is by pausing here and there during and after each one for some intentional reflection. I find that reading in this way, with intentional "pit stops" to process and reflect, helps me dig much deeper into a professional text than I can when I just read it straight through. As you read, try to notice (and even write about):

- How does this person's teaching or setting remind you of your own? How is it different? What do you make of the similarities and differences?
- What surprises you in this teacher's account? Why is it surprising, and what can you learn from the surprise?
- Where do you see the principle that the author identifies coming through in their description of practice?

After you've read all the chapters in this section, try reading back over what you've written in order to consider the group of chapters as a whole. I'll provide some ways of reflecting on your writing at the end of Part II.

Writing for the Soul: Dispelling Shame and Surveillance through Sustaining Writing Practices

Jenell Igeleke Penn

> Writing is embedded in complex social relationships and their appropriate languages.
>
> Everyone has the capacity to write.

Note from Anne

In this chapter, veteran teacher Jenell Igeleke Penn illustrates how she worked with high school students to move from feeling like their writing is "trash" to finding writing important for thinking about things they want to—need to—think about. As she describes her students, their writing, her own transparency, and her own acts of support, she also shows how the principles that "writing is embedded in complex social relationships and their appropriate languages" and that "everyone has the capacity to write" drives her decision making to, first, help students find ideas that they care about and, then, work through their own vulnerability in order to produce pieces of writing they can share with peers.

I'm

Just

That

Good

I could be a rapper if I really tried

Expose all the mannequin and their lies

But I really don't have the time

Too busy keeping up with the rights

Of people my

Age

Color

And size

You should be crowning me

All this thick sensory surrounding me

I'll put you in the center of my world

I swear it's lit

After being in the dark so long

I think I deserve it.

A resounding and collective "Oooohhhhhhhh!" filled the space.

Dominic jumped up from his desk and ran across the class to Maleeyah's desk, his hand balled into a fist and leaned in for the dap.

"You killed it, Maleeyah! Who's next?" he shouted.

"I can't go after that!" Dasia protested.

"C'mon, y'all. This is what it's all about," Dominic responded.

This *is* what it is all about. Though Dominic came into my fourth period eleventh-grade American Humanities class with great experience and confidence in his writing abilities, very few of the other young people in the class did. In fact, when asked about their writing abilities, many responded with comments such as, "My writing is trash" and "I'm not a writer." Maleeyah was one of many juniors in the class who loudly wore this badge. Through these declarations came the echoes of writing positioned as something at which only the esteemed and learned succeed, and, even after engaging in writing together for three months, the badge remained.

For several years, I had struggled to truly engage students in writing. Each year I'd start off the school year teaching students about several lenses (feminist, critical race, queer, historical) they could peer through to think deeply and differently about the texts we read, listened to, and viewed (Kinloch, 2011). From these lenses, students engaged in thoughtful discussions about our class texts, their own lives, and larger world contexts, but they pushed back against creating their own texts. I'd assign several essays: narrative, critical analysis, literary analysis, argumentative. They'd turn them in. I'd pull out my red pen and provide meaningful feedback on the paper *and* the rubric, just like I was taught to do in my teacher preparation program. I'd offer the option of revising, but very few students took me up on the offer to revise a B+ paper. Writing was an action done for the teacher, and once submitted, the piece of writing belonged to the teacher. The students didn't own the writing and they didn't want to grow or talk with me about their writing, let alone with one another.

Writing requires risk taking, and writers have to allow themselves to be open, to be vulnerable. How could I get my kids to allow themselves to be vulnerable? The majority of my students were low income and/or Black youth, and they were not afforded the privilege of choosing to be vulnerable. Historically, Black children have been continuously, intentionally, and undesirably vulnerable to violence, hunger, stereotypes, correction, and surveillance. And, in that space of vulnerability, they've been positioned as adults and/or criminals, and they've been expected to be strong and resilient or have "grit" (Duckworth, 2016; Yeh, 2017). So why would they choose to be vulnerable, especially in schools, a space in which they have experienced so much racial violence and erasure?

Additionally, a common false assumption is that simply being a Black teacher will build connections for Black students. However, systems of oppression and white supremacy are in all of us, and being a Black teacher did not erase the violence associated with being a teacher and so-called progressive teaching practices in my students' lives. In so many school spaces, my students have been told to leave their social vernaculars, their language, and their personal experiences at the door. But how can students connect to school and see the benefits and power of writing if they are asked to strip off and whitewash parts of their identities when they walk through the classroom door?

The Principles document asserts that "Writing is embedded in complex social relationships and their appropriate languages." The difficult and long-standing tensions between students and teachers, between home and school languages, and between Black students and teachers and the systemic structures of oppression present in schooling do not just evaporate because I want students to write: writing, as the Principles state,

> happens in the midst of a web of relationships. . . . Therefore, power relationships are built into the writing situation. In every writing situation, the writer, the reader, and all relevant others live in a structured social order, where some people's words count more than others, where being heard is more difficult for some people than others, where some people's words come true and others' do not. (pp. xii–xiii; all page references to the Principles map to the front matter of this book)

In the midst of these truths, I somehow needed to help my students be free to choose to be vulnerable in my class, and to know that it wasn't solely so that they would do what I ultimately wanted them to do. I needed them to choose to grow as writers because they wanted to grow for themselves and for one another. My students were not connecting when it came to the way I was teaching writing—except on Mondays. Something was happening on Mondays. Something good.

Writing for the Soul: Read-Arounds

On Read-Around Mondays, I saw all of my classes for forty minutes, and I saw each period every other day for blocked periods the remainder of the week. Because of the shortened period on Monday and the ability to see each class, Monday became a great day to explore varied forms of writing. Therefore, each Monday we dedicated the entire class period to read-arounds for forty minutes. Drawing on a practice I learned from Robin Holland through the Columbus Area Writing Project and featured in her book, *Deeper Writing: Quick Writes and Mentor Texts to Illuminate New Possibilities* (2012) and in Linda Christensen's book *Reading, Writing, and Rising Up* (2017), I presented a read-around prompt, one that paired with a mentor or thinking text and offered three options for creative writing. These options connected to our topic for the grading period: American Identity (GP1), American Nightmare (GP2), American Dreaming (GP3), and Using Your American Voice (GP4). Each week we focused on a different read-around. Sometimes the prompt asked students to try out a specific container (e.g., a six-word memoir or a collaborative story); other times, the prompt asked students to address specific themes or topics such as different versions of the American Dream, how musicians respond to oppressions, biases in our perspectives, different metaphors for America, and what students know they know—epistemologies (ways of knowing how we know what we know, what counts as "truth," and where beliefs inform truths) and ontologies (ways of defining and naming categories and characteristics so that we can talk about them) that are typically left out of schools.

When my students wrote, I wrote. When they shared, I shared. When my students asked for feedback or advice on their writing, I asked for feedback and advice on my writing. Everyone shared; not always with the whole group, but everyone wrote because everyone could. It was important for me to model both vulnerability and confidence in writing with my students so that they could see how I asked for help, how the writing process unfolded, and how my writing changed over time. In her book *Black Literate Lives*, Maisha Fisher (2008) argues that English teachers must be "practitioners of the craft" and model and engage in the literacy practices with students. She further argues that taking this stance builds strong community with students and fosters growth. For this new path to work, my students and I had to trust one another. After describing the read-around concept, I discussed with students our expectations as a community of writers. We agreed on three expectations: (1) everyone writes; (2) a writer shares when and what they are ready to share; and (3) feedback is constructive and encourages further development. Often as teachers we set expectations for our students, but we don't embody them ourselves. I knew that if I wanted my students' writing to improve, they needed to care about their writing and see themselves as writers, and for them to see that, I needed to show my own vulnerabilities.

> **Note from Anne**
>
> In keeping with the principle that "writing and reading are related," it is in Jenell's existing practice as a reading teacher that she finds ways to open doors to writing that students had kept closed. Along the way, she and her students form a powerful community of writers who trust one another enough to take chances with their writing—and with each other.

So it was during read-arounds that space was created for the soul and the whole to be present. Most important, no language, no "drama," and no words were off limits, and everyone in the room (classroom aides, visitors, students, intervention specialists, and myself) participated. We encouraged one another to not just write for the soul but to soulfully listen as well. We extended our understanding of reading deeply and differently (Kinloch, 2013), to writing deeply and differently, and to listening deeply and differently. During this particular school year, I lost a child, and my students were aware. Instead of pretending it didn't happen and leaving my "personal drama" at the door, I wrote about my pain. In *Teaching to Transgress*, hooks (1994) writes:

> When education is the practice of freedom, students are not the only ones who are asked to share, to confess. Engaged pedagogy does not seek simply to empower students. Any classroom that employs a holistic model of learning will also be a place where teachers grow, and are empowered by the process. That empowerment cannot happen if we refuse to be vulnerable while encouraging students to take risks. (p. 21)

I not only became a practitioner of the craft with my students and, therefore, part of the writing and revision group, but I also confessed what made me feel joyful or broken. Thus, I positioned myself as both vulnerable and empowered by the writing process. I extended this same space for my students. One particular week I shared a prompt that asked students to explore the concept of "home." One student, Jason, wrote about feeling at home when he smokes marijuana. Some educators would censor students' writing at this point. However, for a student who needed intensive writing help and was opening up for the first time all year, I did not want to squash his engagement. Instead, I saw this as an opportunity to engage Jason, to move him toward wellness, and show him that he could write. To say that his piece could not be part of the class would have been counter to the com-

Note from Anne

Jenell and the other adults in her classroom enact a simple yet challenging piece of wisdom from the earliest process-oriented writing teachers: write along with your students. It is so valuable, yet so difficult to do. Practically, it's hard not to claim that time for recordkeeping, managing interruptions, or organizing the next activity. Emotionally, it's hard to slow down enough. To take your attention off of the students for long enough. Or to get vulnerable enough. Even when not bravely sharing an experience of grief like Jenell's, writing authentically tends to take us to some tender places. We don't always know whether we can trust students with that, either. But when we can, not only do we get to model writing practices, but we also get to model vulnerability. Jenell's students show us why this is such a gift.

munity we had created. It was part of him; therefore, it was part of us. While not every teacher would or, depending on circumstances, could make the same choice, I chose to prioritize my concern about evoking writing, any writing at all, from Jason over my concern about how my decision might look from the outside. This is what happens when, as Anne Haas Dyson (1993) puts it, we make the curriculum "permeable," where students can enter and influence it and where it can enter and influence the lives and minds of students: once you engage students so authentically, they also will engage the work authentically, and they will bring with them all that is real to them—including things we as teachers are not always ready for.

Vulnerability: Letting Themselves Be Seen

It was through this Monday read-around practice that I realized that for my students to grow in all aspects of writing, they had to let themselves be seen as writers, as creators. In assigning writing the first half of the year (and every year prior), I had mainly focused on the skills and knowledge the state said my students needed to have and know. My overall curriculum was grounded in culturally responsive pedagogy (Ladson-Billings, 1992), and students engaged in social justice capstone projects, but when it came to writing, the things I was asking them to do were not truly responsive, sustaining, or led by them. In contrast to the vibrant, student-centered, deep engagement with issues that mattered to students during read-around, when it was time for writing, I reverted to teacher-assigned prompts that resulted in rather listless products. Read-Around Mondays were great, but the practice stayed in the Monday slot, and students never received sustained meaningful feedback on or continuous time for creation and revision of their read-arounds. But this is when I saw students come alive. This is where they saw themselves as writers, saw that each and every one of them could write something. This needed to be the norm in my class.

So I committed to making a change. I hemmed and hawed over my decision to forego a focus on standardized and formal writing as the most important as we moved into the second half of the school year and instead put my energies into writing for the soul. Rather than a final analysis paper, the final project focused on read-around. Considering teacher evaluations, I was terrified. What if what I did set students back? What if they don't score well on the ACT? What if, what if, what if? I looked into the deep pool of what ifs and jumped.

I wanted to push students to really see and embody the writing process and to challenge myself to strengthen my students' writing skills utilizing different methods. Instead of moving to read-around every day (a new prompt, a new start), I shifted to developing a piece of writing (often begun in read-around) into something more polished, with each student taking ownership so that we could continue to build trust and confidence in our writing skills and in one another. I decided to have students choose one of their own pieces from the year, and I charged them with perfecting the chosen piece into something complete and publishable. I encouraged them to choose one that would best showcase their growth and talent. Once the students had chosen their pieces (e.g., blog posts, fan fiction, poems, editorials), I provided them with the following list of tasks:

- Choose a container and make it shine.
- Propose below who will be in your group. There must be at least three people in a group and no more than five.
- Read work aloud during group meetings.
- Revise and edit one another's work.
- Provide timely feedback to other writers.
- Assist in research and revision.
- Participate in a variety of revision exercises.
- Provide group members updated pieces to read and hear.

Allowing students to organize themselves into writing groups was a critical step in showing students that I believed in their writing abilities. I was demonstrating that I believed not only in their abilities to write but also in their abilities to support one another's writing, both emotionally and academically. Part of the writing process is revising and writing with others, and for this to become clearer, I needed to share the pedagogical hat. We had learned from one another all year as a whole-class read-around group, but I was the sole facilitator. Now I wanted them to teach and learn from one another in smaller read-around groups. I emphasized the importance of supporting one another through the writing process by providing meaningful feedback, listening ears, and creative ideas. Additionally, I looked for evidence of active and collaborative revision within the writing groups each week.

At first, students resisted.

"What's the template for writing something like this the right way?"

"Why do I have to have him read my writing? You're the teacher!"

"I don't know how to fix this!"

"I'm tired of fixing this."

It seemed that assigning the read-around process and products as the final project somehow triggered certain hardwired anxieties and fears about writing. The project was going to be graded, and graded meant judging, unchosen vulnerability, and surveillance. It was hard not to abandon ship, but I wanted students to see that to be writers, they didn't have to rely solely on me. They already were writers and they already knew so much about writing. Writing isn't easy, but just because it isn't easy didn't mean they couldn't do it. So I did two things. First, I led students through the assignment (which I had decided without them) and we co-constructed expectations. Second, at least once a week I led a mini-lesson on some topic related to writing that the students found challenging: comma usage, writing with metaphors and allusions, parallel structure, setting development, the art of peer revision. Sometimes I led the class; sometimes Mr. Johnson, our intervention specialist, led the class; and sometimes the students led the class. But, no matter how hard it seemed, we kept writing and we kept progressing.

At the end of the year, we held our final read-around session. This session was about honoring the writing we had produced and celebrating our collective growth. Deciding to make this change midyear was scary. I'm a planner, and my plans for the year were set! So I was reluctant, but I came to understand that writing instruction wasn't about me. It was about my students and what they needed. And the fire in my chest whenever I heard them share on Read-Around Mondays meant I needed to prioritize their languages and interests. I chose my students. I chose to honor their languages and their interests. They could and should own and command writing; it did not command them. They could insert themselves into the conversations that were important to them. This is not to say that our other writing assignments were unimportant and would be forgotten, but I needed to reframe them in ways that allowed students to own the writing and the evaluation process. Writing is not about shame, surveillance, and correction, but about celebration, growth, and inclusion of our whole selves.

This example of a poem read by one student at the end of the year illustrates this point:

To be American is to be the black bird.

The bird that soars the sky; over the strange fruit dangling, hanging, melting off the trees with cocoa brown leaves onto the dark green grass left there for several days – in and out.

To be American is to use the "American Language."

To be Ebonics as proper grammar. To speak how I was raised. To slang and slur my words. To use words like "cuz," "ya'll," and "finna" because I can.

Not because I do not have the mental capacity to do otherwise.
To be American is to learn about my people, culture, and lifestyle in-
    stead of a whitewashed copy.
Like the things you learn in history books.
To be American is to use Ebonics because it is culture – not remedial.

I argued at the outset of this chapter that the ways I work with student writers in my setting are grounded in the principle that "writing is embedded in complex social relationships and their appropriate languages." This fact, and the fact of schools' long-term complicity in silencing student voices rather than elevating them, poses a special challenge to writing teachers like me and other teachers working with students from backgrounds that are too often marginalized and oppressed. Yet, another principle opens possibility: Everyone has the capacity to write; writing can be taught; and teachers can help students become better writers. The question is, are we paying attention, and have we told our students otherwise?

Note from Anne

This student's poem makes the point, just as his teacher has in this chapter, that "writing is embedded in complex social relationships and their appropriate languages." I love how this student uses language to talk back to language, not only in his direct comments about Ebonics but also in the way he wraps images like "strange fruit" and "whitewashed" in the same Standard English that he names as having positioned Ebonics as "remedial."

Chapter Four

Expanding Creative Writing to Collaborative Genres

Paula Uriarte

> Writing grows out of many purposes.
>
> Writing is a process.

Note from Anne

Paula Uriarte describes how her juniors and seniors in Boise, Idaho, who have elected to take an advanced creative writing course, typically see writing as a solitary activity. However, most writing that adults do involves collaboration. Writing in unexpected genres helps Paula's students to experience collaborative writing in genres they typically wouldn't encounter in school. Here she describes an example that shows how her students enact two of the principles in the Principles document: writing for many purposes and writing as a process.

My Advanced Creative Writing class, juniors and seniors who have already taken two semester-long prerequisites, is mapping out character connections on the whiteboard as we prepare a Murder Mystery Dinner for a group of teacher-leaders who provide professional development for other teachers around Idaho. The students pitched ideas in small groups for what our story should be, and now we've gone with The Night Howler's Ski Lodge. Here's the backstory as written by the students:

> Klyde Poe is a banker who has been stealing from his clients. He has a religious conversion and decides he needs to atone for his mistakes, so he invites his clients to the Night Howler's Ski Lodge to give them back their money and treat them to a great weekend to make amends.

Today we are making sure all of the connections characters have to each other are clear so that it's hard to trace who the real killer is but not impossible. This is a large group for this kind of work—twenty students, all creative people— and you can tell there's a little frustration but also a deep desire to figure out this web of characters.

Creative Writing courses at my school often tend to attract students who want to just write and be left alone to do so. Many of them see the work as solitary, and they like it that way. While I hate to generalize, I have come to expect students who might be described as "angsty"—who like to write abstract and often morose poetry, students who love science fiction, and lately a group of girls who are devoted to "fan fic" from *Supernatural* to the Harry Potter series and anything I can possibly imagine in between. Most of them want to write the Great American Novel or try to make their living as a writer. Some just like to write and want a space to do so. Regardless of where they come from, they are not used to writing anything collaboratively. But statistically, very few of them will eventually be in a position where they write fiction or poetry, solitarily, to pay the bills. If part of my job is to mentor students into the practice of the discipline, I need them to see the more realistic possibilities of the kinds of work they could do to make a living as a writer. Newspapers, magazines, television shows, websites, escape rooms, gaming companies all have teams of writers, not one, lone cigarette-smoking, whisky-swilling, typewriter-punching icon. This means students need to experience the kinds of writing they might have to do. In this chapter, I show how I have worked with my Creative Writing students to write in many genres, in keeping with the principles articulated in the NCTE Principles document that "Writing grows out of many purposes" and "Writing is a process."

The group of writers who planned the Murder Mystery Dinner described above were sophomores through seniors of diverse identities, including gender expressions. Most students in this group were incredibly talented writers. While they started the year with definite preferences for certain genres, they were willing to try new forms and were often surprised at their success. This success led them to take more risks as the year went on. These identities were always at play in the writing and even influenced some of our discussions of direction for our Murder Mystery Dinner.

Writing in Creative Writing: From Journals to Real-World Genres

A typical day in the class begins with a journal prompt. I liken this writing to playing scales or doing voice warm-ups in music or stretching before a run. In our introductory classes, these prompts are usually tied to skills. If we are looking at characterization, they may be writing character sketches from pictures or trying several different ways to describe the same character or showing the age of a character without using any numbers. If we are working on plot, they might begin with a loose plot structure (man and woman get into a taxicab) and, over the course of the week, write different versions of a story that fits that plot. Often these prompts come with a mentor text of the kind of writing they will do. I ask students to write at least one line in response to the prompt, but it's a rare occasion that students don't try what we are doing. When we finish, they are given the option to share. This is always an option for journal prompts. I often name one or two things I see the writer doing, but for the most part we show appreciation instead of critique. I try most of the time to write with my students, and sometimes I will share. Every year it is a goal for me to write with them *every day*, and every year I fail.

In time, the students take over the task of creating journal prompts.

Note from Anne

Of course, prompts are themselves a genre, one that students have interacted with many times by the time they reach Paula Uriarte's course. The difference here is that Paula helps the students engage the prompts not only as instructions for success in a school task but also as examples in a genre, one whose features can be recognized and analyzed. This work with the genre of prompts lays groundwork for the more explicit genre analysis in which they will next engage.

They write prompts for our journals on index cards and someone different draws each day. They base their prompt writing on our investigation of the prompts they liked in the first-year class. We discuss those favorites and why students liked them. Eventually, students develop a shared set of criteria for good prompts, such as "open-ended, but not too open," "gets a variety of responses," and "intriguing." They know their audience well, because students in the class will actually write to one another's prompts. These experiments in journal prompt writing serve an important purpose: teaching the class to be audiences for one another's work and developing shared understandings of what different audiences (in this case, creative writing students!) might need.

As Creative Writing progresses, students write nonfiction, fiction, and poetry, always working from mentor texts to identify what they might like to imitate in their own writing. Every six weeks, they take a piece to publication, drawing on feedback from small groups to revise, then reading from an Author's Chair in a celebration. After these experiences, and after trust and collaborative skills have developed, we turn to Murder Mystery Dinners and Escape Rooms as collaborative writing challenges.

Close-up: Murder Mysteries and Escape Rooms

None of the students had ever participated in a Murder Mystery Dinner, so we started our work by playing the game "How to Host a Teen Mystery: Hot Times at Hollywood High," which my friend Chris had found at a thrift store. Murder Mystery Dinners are events where a group of people come together and role-play a character in a particular scenario where some mystery is solved in the course of the evening. Usually there is a backstory or inciting incident, and then clues are revealed throughout the meal or event that lead to the final reveal of who perpetrated the crime. It's like a live version of *Clue*. I also shared with students a dinner I put together for my stepdaughter for her birthday— a "Talent Show," in which characters were created and assigned based on the family and friends who attended. Like the "Hollywood High" example, we used "Talent Show" as another mentor text. In addition to having students analyze features of these two mentor texts, I was also able to model process using "Talent Show," sharing how I made decisions when creating it, what went well, and what I would do differently for the future.

A friend suggested his group of teacher-leaders as the audience for our murder mystery night. The students loved the idea of the project, especially having a live audience of real teachers at the other end who would be playing the mystery. We created shared docs and folders, which not only made it easy for us to collaborate, but as one student said, "Then later we can play it with our friends and families." Over a four-week period, we played our mentor text game, deconstructed its components, pitched ideas for backstory, voted on one idea, and then started creating characters. All of this we deliberated using what we knew or could assume about our target audience.

Note from Anne

I think this step of locating an audience is key to the success Paula had with this project. How many times have we asked students to write something for an audience, yet we and they both knew that the writing wouldn't actually be read by that audience? We up the stakes—but also the potential for meaningful engagement with a writing task—when we set students up as writers for an actual audience.

Our mentor text had descriptions for each character in three rounds that included "Hidden Truths" and "Gossip about Others." To fit our large audience, we had to create a larger number of characters than our mentor text had, allowing for sets of partners to work on a character. Once we had a round of ideas for each character, we came back together in the whole group to see how each idea fit with the other characters. Students did a lot of mapping on the whiteboards and had to revise their ideas based on what was happening with other characters. These conversations were powerful to observe; students sometimes had to let an idea go, and at other times they were visibly excited as they brought characters together and developed more complicated story lines. This process included constant discussion and revision and some passionate but productive arguments. We also had a hitch close to the end when our teacher-leader group increased by one and we needed a new character. This sent the students back to the whiteboard and forced one more set of revisions. As we put the package together, student strengths came out in the creation of invitations, directions for game play, and the design of the box filled with the evening's props and clues. Even the format of our mentor text was updated by the use of technology.

Our mystery mentor text came with a cassette tape to narrate the game (and luckily one of our media specialists still had a tape player in the library for emergencies); updating this, our students who were also in the Video Broadcasting course gained access to the green screen to film an opening. A video created by the students (https://www.youtube.com/watch?v=Y82o8m4YMX8) introduced the mystery to game players: during the opening, Klyde dies, and the guests must figure out how he died while role-playing their given characters. We did a dry run, then finally handed the student-illustrated box of invites, props, and clue envelopes to my teacher friends for their June meeting.

After their mystery night, the teacher-participants wrote thank-yous, most of them as their character, and took pictures for us. Some comments included: "Thanks for a dark and twisted time. The carnage was excellent." "This was a great experience. Who knew I could possibly commit murder?" "Thanks for helping me get in touch with my inner actor!" "Wow! So wonderfully written and organized. I never would have spent this much time working on it, but I will take it." Everything had gone smoothly, and the clues and plot were easy to follow. The reveal was not obvious, and the teacher coaching team was really able to do some bonding through participating in the game before they started the hard work they had to do.

The following school year, I was introduced to Escape Rooms, which have exploded in popularity. Essentially, a group of people surrender their cell phones and are "locked" in a room for an hour with a series of puzzles, varying from wordplay to ciphers, to solve in order to escape the room before the time is up. The rooms have a theme and a backstory and there are many variations. Some Escape Rooms use actors to narrate the story, and then take participants into the room. Some open the door and let players in to figure out what is happening. Most of

June 2016: Idaho coaching network Night Howler's Ski Lodge participants Jackie Miller (Mary Sanguinum), Brandon Bolyard (Hank), and Emily Morgan (Black Star) in character.

them have some form of help if the players are missing clues. This also seemed a great opportunity for students to collaboratively create. I did some online research and found a skeleton of ideas for creation at https://lockpaperscissors.co . I also contacted a local Escape Room and asked if the writers would come talk to my students. I was planning to then go online to find a preestablished Escape and then create one myself as a mentor text. But the owners of Boise Escape suggested that instead of Boise Escape coming to my classroom, I bring my students to them to experience an Escape for themselves, *free of charge*. This was an incredibly generous gesture, as it's about $28 a person to attend in normal circumstances. After our experiences with the "Lost City of Z" and "Tick, Tock, BOOM!," my students then collaboratively created "Escape the Speakeasy" and "Escape the Drawing Room" experiences for other teachers and staff in our building. We started by identifying the characteristics of the genre we experienced and then brainstorming ideas for a theme. We had several possibilities, but it happened that many of the students had been reading *The Great Gatsby* or *Pride and Prejudice*, so there were campaigns for themes stemming from both novels. In the end, we decided to do two small groups because we couldn't agree as a class on one theme.

Note from Anne

Conceiving of writing as a process does not mean prescribing a specific process to students. Instead, it means helping them learn to adapt processes they've used before to new situations and suggesting actions they might take in the process of developing a text that is new to them. More difficult for many of us, it means remaining open to processes our student writers employ that are different from those we have taught or those we might use ourselves, but that are helpful and effective for them.

Note from Anne

Reflection helps writers move from simply doing something to realizing what its effects were and in what situations they might wish to do it again. Paula Uriarte supports her students in reflection via an oral debrief after the class has tried something new or test-run a draft.

The Escape Room presented challenges different from those of the Murder Mystery Dinner. The students quickly created a scenario that "locked" participants in but then had to think about the physical space of the classroom and how it could be transformed between Escapes (and quickly), as well as how they could monitor what was happening, in order to provide clues to participants since we didn't have the advantage of surveillance video. This problem-solving not only forced them to pay close attention to details, but they also had to shift their narratives at times to accommodate the changes. For example, the Speakeasy group decided they would have "bartenders" stay in the room so they could provide clues when needed. The Drawing Room centered on the story of Eleanor, whose crazy uncle was forcing her to marry someone she didn't like. That group's solution was to have Eleanor locked in the room as well, and when the participants struggled, she surreptitiously text-messaged a colleague in the next room, who would slip note card clues under the adjoining door, much like what students had seen in the Boise Escape experience we used as our mentor text. The note card clues required some impromptu thinking and for the clue-writing students to really know and understand their story. When students were working on their rooms, they were alternately at their tables brainstorming together or hunched over the laptop composing an activity or clue. When individuals finished a piece, they brought it to the whole group for feedback and any necessary revision. The process was embedded in the activity.

Creating a variety of clues proved difficult at times, so students did some online research as well. They wrote poems that held clues, created riddles, and made ciphers with books and their titles. We ordered locks and borrowed boxes and props from other teachers in the building.

Finally, we ran the rooms. One of the groups escaped at the last minute, and the other didn't. We then debriefed what we could have done differently and looked at surveys we gave our participants. This helped to demonstrate to my writers the importance of feedback and reflection before and after revision.

Teaching from Principles

The students who select my creative writing courses have often come with a pre-conception that the only reason to engage in creative writing is for self-expression and that the only way to do so is alone. In the teaching I have described here, I have tried to broaden their experiences in creative writing to include a variety of purposes. As the Principles document states,

> Since writers outside school have many different purposes beyond demonstrating ac-countability and they use more diverse genres of writing, it is important that students have experiences within school that teach them how writing differs with purpose, audience, and other elements of the situation. (pp. xi–xii)

Much of our work together aims for this goal. In experimenting with prompts and in creating games, we are also developing ways of understanding our audiences and of understanding why genres have the particular features that they do.

Further, my efforts to engage students in writing as collaborators in unfamil-iar genres also stems from my belief in the principle that "writing is a process." It was really easy when I started teaching Creative Writing, an elective class, to find "fun" things for my students to do that kept their attention and got them writ-ing, but I started to see so much potential in making every activity applicable to a broader understanding of what writing is and is capable of doing for a student as a communicator, and ultimately as a human being. I could have just assigned a game, or assigned them to create some writing prompts. But by engaging students in collaborative writing, I am able to foreground process in my teaching, looking beyond the product they are creating to the processes they are using to create it. When coauthoring, they are forced to speak aloud about the decisions they are making and why, making processes explicit. From there, students can support one another through those processes, and I can supply needed instruction along the way. As a writer, I've always had a sense that giving my students "formulas" was a bad idea, as five paragraphs with a three-part thesis didn't look anything like the writing they would see anywhere else. I've got overheads from early in my teaching of hamburgers, trains, and sandwiches as metaphors for what an essay should look like, and I had been to various "trainings" to teach me how to be a better writing instructor—some better than others and some that were downright horrible. Since I began working with the Boise State Writing Project in 2005, I've been trying to move toward a more conscious competence about what I am doing and why. The idea that "creative" writing is different from other writing is erroneous; the process we go through in creative writing applies in any writing course.

Many of my Writing Project colleagues also validated some of my core beliefs about writing: Teachers should write along with their students since modeling is an integral part of the process. Students should be given the opportunity to see good and different models, a belief that was reinforced by an elementary colleague who introduced me to mentor texts. Students should write—a lot—and for many reasons, and choice should be involved whenever possible.

The most visible differences from my earlier teaching are in the genres in which students write, including the mysteries and escapes I have described here. Deborah Dean's *Genre Theory* (2008) was an important work in this shift. Dean's work gave me a starting point for conversations about genre with my students and moved me to start with genre in any writing situation—what are the typical characteristics of the form we are writing if it is a genre familiar to students? If it isn't, what models will I provide that will help students see not only the typical characteristics but also the ways that various authors may have manipulated the traditional characteristics for some effect? What will their assignment be that seems relevant to current kinds of writing in the world, optimizes choice, and gives them an authentic audience? What will I write and how will I share my choices with students in the process of our work?

In all of the courses I teach, students become investigators instead of followers. When I give students models of the kinds of writing we do, they name what they see as characteristics of the genre and effective moves in the writing. With practice, students imitate those characteristics and often manipulate them for effect. My goal is to get them to a place where they feel confident enough to make bold choices in their own work and articulate their reasons for doing so—not only in their semester in Creative Writing, but also in their lives writing in all kinds of situations and genres.

Embracing Messy Writing Rituals

Amanda Micheletty

> Writing is a tool for thinking.
>
> Assessment of writing involves complex, informed, human judgment.

Note from Anne

Amanda Micheletty teaches at Riverstone International School in Boise, Idaho, an independent school with grades 10–12 in its high school. Here, she shows how one aspect of her teaching builds on the principle that writing is a tool for thinking. She takes us from classroom routines—things we do again and again—to rituals—things we do again and again that are imbued with meaning by and carry express meaning for members of a community. With these rituals, her students move from framing their work as bound by a test to framing it as important in a wider way. In doing so, they also show how (as the Principles document states) assessment of writing involves informed human judgment.

We are two weeks into a unit with Kurt Vonnegut's *Slaughterhouse-Five*. Absorbed in the rhythm of our reading ritual, students talk to one another in small groups: some passively, some with a seriousness characteristic of our community of high-achieving students. I walk from group to group, noting the bright spots in their conversations. Their writer's notebooks are open: two simple columns and three rows labeled "True," "Troubling," and "Beautiful"—and beside each label, a personally selected quote from the assigned chapters.

The busyness of this opening small-group discussion is comforting to me now, having spent the first week of our unit in the tense, often frustrated conversation or silence of students who felt they were being handed a raw deal with this particular book. Because students knew from the beginning of the unit that they would have to respond to *Slaughterhouse-Five* for their International Baccalaureate (IB) diploma, a challenging diploma program combining a slate of advanced courses with external examinations, they have built up a kind of collective resistance to it. They have voiced a concern that the complexity of the text could inhibit their future IB score and that the writing they have to submit to outside examiners, a "creative response" that demonstrates a deep understanding of the work, could be compromised. The phrase "You're torturing us, Ms. Micheletty" has been offered to me more than once.

But today marks a shift in student thinking. Today, the conversations I overhear center on the trouble and tensions of the novel, not gripes with being IB students. And their writer's notebooks are guiding these independent conversations.

Having circled the room and observed the natural lull in student-led discussion, I call out for any insights, things shared by the students themselves or by their partners. A number of students raise their hands, pointing to places in the text and in their conversation that made them think, that connect to what they believe to be true and troubling and beautiful. In a whirl of conversation that lasts much longer than I planned for, I consider how much closer we are now to our essential question for the unit: "What changes us?" Without hesitation, students return to their notebooks, and the second part of the ritual is in full swing. For the next ten minutes, students write freely and sometimes fiercely about a single quote or element of their group discussion, struggling to make sense of their own insights and criteria.

Writing to Move beyond Assessment

Riverstone International School is a small, independent school in Boise, Idaho. The group of students described in the narration above are juniors in high school and first-year candidates of the Diploma Programme for the International Baccalaureate. And while the IB prides itself on the openness and global perspective of its curriculum, the very nature of high-stakes external exams and prescribed writing assessments (culminating in students' senior year) results in a pretty narrow perception of the Language and Literature course I teach—particularly when it comes to reading and writing. As a result, Riverstone students become fixated on IB scores, IB rubrics, IB expectations, and IB lingo (and who can blame them?). They want to know what their audience, *the IB* (more than me or their peers or any authentic audience of choice), wants. They collectively reverberate the same questions: What specific meaning am I to make of this book? What do I have to write and say (*and think*) to get the right IB score?

I know that many teachers in many assessment contexts—whether systems of state exams, SAT prep, Advanced Placement, or Honors programs—confront similar ideologies about thinking and learning: that there is *a* way to write about a given text. And while I appreciate that my students, for the most part, have goals as learners, teaching to expand such a limited lens of what writing and thinking about other texts can do is challenging. Within the constraints of the IB program, I find myself asking the following questions: How do I help my students authentically join the conversation that a text invites them into? And how can using writing as "a tool for thinking" (as named in the Principles document) help them discover what they really care about?

In my many failed attempts at addressing the tension of these questions, I have started to shift my approaches to teaching writing and reading. I have found that grounding my instruction in the principle that writing *is* thinking offers opportunities for students to really engage in writing as a process and not just as a final demonstration of proficiency or talent. Writing to think has helped my students find ways into authentic responses to texts within and outside of the prescriptive, programmatic assessment purposes that can restrict their sense of themselves as writers and learners.

In focusing on writing as thinking, I have both developed and borrowed different rituals in reading, note-taking, journaling, and drafting that help students to dismantle some of the thinking reinforced by assessment-driven curricula. These rituals help students read and write from a more empowered stance that privileges their unique interests and insights into a text than is possible in an authoritative directive from the IB or from me. In this chapter, I describe how claiming writing as "a tool for thinking" offers up space for students to approach prescriptive

Note from Anne

I had experiences similar to Amanda's when I taught high school Honors courses, and I still have them now, as a university professor working with undergraduates who are accustomed to total immersion in points systems, real-time electronic gradebooks, high-stakes testing as a publicly valued symbol of success, and a sense of scarcity of available places in college and in jobs after college. I am encouraged by colleagues like Amanda, as well as those like Sarah Donovan (ethicalela.com), who has chronicled her explorations in un-grading and self-evaluation by her students.

assessments with a clearer grasp of their own intentions, a more nuanced sense of audience, and a willingness to prioritize their own interests as writers. And while final, high-stakes assessments do not disappear from students' concerns, consistently engaging in authentic, messy writing practices that make their thinking visible allows students to see those assessments as less central to their experience as writers and readers.

Writing to Engage with Challenging Texts and Conversations

The reading ritual of noting where in the text students encounter something that is true, troubling, or beautiful was adapted from a protocol that my colleague, Jim Fredricksen, uses with his students at Boise State University. I ask students to collect their reactions to the text as they read, looking specifically for quotes that seem true, troubling, or beautiful. This move alone asks students to position themselves as collaborative responders, in conversation with the text. And it assumes, regardless of the text's complexity or initial appeal, that there is something of value to be found in it, something worthy of their consideration outside of the IB's value system (often reduced to identifying the purpose of authorial choices like symbolism, personification, etc.). In a way, taking these simple notes and then journaling about why they fit a particular, personalized criteria of what is true, troubling, or beautiful to them is also a move toward seeing the text as generative, as something that merits our study and response—not just because it is assigned by a teacher.

Informal Reading and Writing at Work

Next, students use "true, troubling, or beautiful" to journal while they read *Slaughterhouse-Five*. In this part of the ritual, students write informally and without self-censoring about quotes they pulled from the reading, explaining why each was beautiful or troubling or true to them. I emphasize to students that I will never see what they write in this part of their notebooks and that it has no accompanying grade. It is space for them to freely make sense of what they think is important to wrestle with in the text. And while I provide models of my own thinking and how I struggle through naming my criteria for each category or explaining my thoughts about a quote, I really do leave this part of the process unmonitored. This element of the ritual is designed to practice messy, underdeveloped thinking: a space to ask questions, to challenge the author, to express confusion or frustration, to make sense or no sense of their criteria. If students are ever going to get to the point in their writing lives where they trust that writing is a way of thinking, a way of making visible what they are trying to understand, then I should not always have access to that thinking as their teacher. This helps students make connections to the text that are not subject to the authoritative gaze of the International Baccalaureate scorers that I sometimes represent in the minds of students. And so these journals are always a way into their own thinking.

In a reflection that developed out of these informal responses to the text, one initially hesitant student, Olivia, commented on how she made use of the criteria she created in her journal entries. When asked to explain and categorize her criteria, she wrote:

> Music plays an important role within my life, so whenever it was alluded to in the text, I was immediately intrigued. The reason that I found the quotes that mentioned music to be beautiful was because I personally think of music as some sort of divine beauty. So, while the quotes may not have beautiful subject matter, I was able to find elegance within them because of their allusions to music.
>
> By discussing music, I think that Vonnegut made his characters' scenarios more relatable, and almost more palpable because music is something that all of his readers have experienced. For this reason, the readers can understand what the characters are experiencing.

I can see the kind of work this does for students in another example reflection my student, Ian, wrote, born out of his unmonitored journal entries. He drafted this part of his reflection as a letter to Kurt Vonnegut:

> The narrator brings to light truths that just couldn't be expressed by Billy. They are often much more blunt and direct. . . . A solid example of this is when Valencia said to Billy, "'You must have secrets about the war. Or, not secrets, I guess, but things you don't want to talk about'" (154). It is kind of like, yeah, no kidding. I think you [Kurt Vonnegut] did a great job showing people one of the problems with Post Traumatic Stress Disorder (PTSD). Even when people know that you might have PTSD they will still bring it up. It is such a rude and nosy thing to do.
>
> I personally believe that you should never ask a soldier about their experience at war. That is where the truth lies in this quote. I have a cousin named Brock. He was in the National Guard when he was called up to active duty and sent to Iraq. I get scared whenever he brings up anything about his experience in the army because I don't want to trigger any sort of PTSD for him. [. . .] No one knows if Brock had an uneventful time in Iraq or if he killed children by just following orders. We won't ever ask either that's what is so shocking about this quote the fact that it is such a contradiction to what we should be doing. That is what makes it so true for me. You applied that masterfully in this novel over and over again. It made us really question as a reader what is right and what is wrong.

What I see in this reflection and in Olivia's are students grappling with their own thinking, trying to make sense of why they read something in a particular way. In doing so, they engage in valuable writing that is not a final product. In his reflective letter, Ian positions himself in intentional conversation with the author

Note from Anne

These experiences with informal writing while students read show how Amanda Micheletty's teaching draws not only on the principle of "writing as a tool for thinking" but also on the idea that "writing and reading are related." The students' reading makes their writing possible, of course, but what may be less obvious is how their writing has in turn enriched their reading.

of the text. This is a move I ask my students to make all the time in more formal contexts, but here, in the safer space of his writer's notebook, Ian does it in a way that makes sense to him as an independent writer. His letter to Vonnegut helps me understand how he is owning his stake in a bigger conversation about PTSD, and he does it by practicing the skills and strategies he developed in informal writing rituals: he integrates direct quotes from the novel, speaks back to the text with the authority of his personal experience, and makes meaningful judgments about the "masterful" work of the author himself. Later on in the semester, both Ian and Olivia use the writing from their notebooks to develop polished, final works, but their engagement with the earlier processes of writing to think and discover inspires writing that surprises and excites me.

Writing to Build Agency

In her final response, Olivia used the quotes she categorized as "beautiful" to develop a television script that imagined a therapy session between Kurt Vonnegut and a persona like herself. In this example, I can see her integrating quotes in creative ways and speaking to particular authorial choices that matter most to her as a reader. Here is a glimpse of a scene later in the script:

> Olivia relaxes slightly more into the chair, and Kurt takes a swig from his cup of coffee.

Kurt So, the fourth way of seeing beauty within your own life, and also within my text, is to recognize what makes life worth living.

> Olivia smiles excitedly.

Olivia So for me, that would be music.

Kurt Sure. For Billy, however, that might be something closer to Death. For example . . .

> *Kurt turns glassy eyed in her direction.* "When he opened his eyes, he was on the bottom of the pool, and there was beautiful music everywhere. He lost consciousness, but the music went on. . . ."

Olivia So, there in the text, you were trying to show the beauty within death by connecting it to a different beautiful concept, which was music?

Kurt To an extent, yes. But I was also juxtaposing the themes of music, which symbolizes life, and death, which symbolizes, well . . . you know.

Olivia *(pausing slowly)* You're saying . . . that even when times may seem dark, we can always find something that is beautiful, something that is worth living for.

Kurt For you, that would be music. Don't ever lose it.

      Olivia exhales heavily, and Kurt downs the remains of his coffee, glancing down at his watch.

In a similar vein, Ian wrote a short story after considering his personal connection to Vonnegut's arguments about PTSD. In it, he explores this idea with a more marginal character and mirrors Vonnegut's structural and stylistic choices. Here is a brief look at the opening paragraphs of his story:

> After Dresden, Lazzaro went back to a happy little home in Santa Barbara. His mom died a week after Lazzaro joined the army. She caught a vicious case of pneumonia, she was only 43. So it goes.
>
>   His dad was a drunk. He hardly noticed his eldest son was gone for over a year. Darn shame, each one of Lazzaro's brothers suffered their father's wrath. Lazzaro couldn't be concerned with his brothers' wellbeing. He had been in the war. The suffering would make them who they are.

These examples reflect writers taking increasing agency in their writing. Too often, in test-writing situations, student writers will speak very conservatively about the texts they are asked to analyze, fearful of being "wrong," or so focused on producing "correct" essay structures as framed by the constraints of test writing that content itself takes a backseat as they compose. Yet in both of these examples, Olivia and Ian are using the thinking developed in their writer's notebooks to create nuanced and authentic responses to the text.

From Assessment to Thinking: Engaging Principles

These experiences in my classroom help to illustrate the relationship between two of the Principles. "Assessment of writing involves complex, informed, human judgment," and its purpose should be to gain information about and/or make judgments about students' writing skills and the quality of their products. When assessment becomes its own end for student writers, the heart of this principle is lost, and when that happens it is hard for students to approach writing for other purposes. However, in the cases described here, students have been able to move beyond their concerns about assessment to experience how "writing is a tool for thinking" as well.

While both of these writing activities meet the requirements of a particular IB assessment, what is most exciting to me as their teacher is that students are writing about what they care about. These students usually begin with a focus on assessment not only as a tool for evaluating their performance but also (and more consequently) as the entire purpose of writing instruction itself. We are learning this, they reason, so that we can do well on the test. Yet here, students have moved forward, at least a little. They are starting to practice what discerning readers do when they read a text—whether they like that text or not. They are grappling with questions of the mind and engaging in the same processes of journaling and note-taking that expert writers use to arrive at the writing of their own interests. And though both of these students are IB diploma bound, they are also freeing themselves up to be the kinds of thinkers and writers they want to be.

Disrupting Texts: Principled Writing Instruction for Advocacy and Argument

Lyschel Shipp

Writing and reading are related.

Writing is a tool for thinking.

Writing is embedded in complex social relationships
and their appropriate languages.

Note from Anne

From song lyrics, to Ralph Waldo Emerson, to Coates's *Between the World and Me*, Lyschel Shipp's diverse group of students at Central High School in Macon, Georgia, analyze and make texts in many genres, written for many purposes. Then they disrupt and transform these texts to engage others and to use writing for their own agendas. Not only does Lyschel describe the work her students did but she also shares how she came to the teaching practices that support her students.

Rise Up

The bell rings as the students flood the halls in anticipation of their next class. They are ushered along by the daily school transition music playing over the intercom. Today's song is the most powerful one I've heard all semester: Andra Day belting out melodies, and her words mimicking the graceful movements of pirouettes and praise dance. These are lyrics that move you, energize the spirit inside of you, and empower you to rise in spite of challenges and circumstance. We are nearing the end of school, and the lyrics are resonating—fueling emotions, encouraging sing-alongs in both euphonious and cacophonous keys, but mostly telling a story all too familiar: *"You're broken down and tired of living life on a merry go round. And you can't find the fighter, but I see it in you so we gonna walk it out"* ("Rise Up"). The students at Central High School are fighters. They fight with their hearts—often out of necessity, emboldened by the exigency of survival, obliged by the spoken and unspoken rules that govern their lives. They even fight when they don't want to, and because of this they are undeniably resilient and ultimately deserving of all the compassion and power that education can offer.

One of our most powerful practices is writing. For us, it is a transformative experience rooted in authentic stories, critical assessment and commentary of the world around us, and deep-seated in personal reflection. This chapter explores the ways in which my students and I used writing to empower ourselves and others. It is a reflection of NCTE's *Professional Knowledge for the Teaching of Writing* principles "Writing and reading are related," "Writing is a tool for thinking," and" Writing is embedded in complex social relationships and their appropriate languages." Here you will see examples of how we used writing to discuss texts we've read, to question situations and circumstances, and to reflect on who we are as writers and as people—analyzing our academic and personal growth. At the closing of the school year, we measured just how far we had journeyed, but with Lewis Carroll in mind, before we can come to the end, we must "begin at the beginning."

Disrupting Texts for Advocacy and Argument

I stared anxiously into their curious faces on the second day of school. Eyebrows arched in question marks of inquisitiveness when I boldly ask, "What does it mean to be an American?" It was an introductory question to our eleventh-grade American Literature and Writing course, but also a critical question in the evaluation of the literary canon. Who and what would we be reading this school year, and how would these students—Americans—see themselves reflected in the texts? In what ways would we disrupt the canon, engage in culturally relevant learning, and find, craft, or share our voices—voices of Black, Brown, and White students who have experienced poverty, trauma, and limited access to educational resources? These aren't isolated concerns prompted by a deep reflection of the American experience but, rather, lingering questions that students sometimes silently grapple with every year. "What *does* it mean to be an American?" I asked the students to write their responses on the board, a daunting task for some, but eventually waves of students found their way to the front. Their responses revealed both pride in a country they were born in and resistance to oppressive structures that admittedly created hindrances in their lives. Being an American meant *freedom* and *discrimination*. It was the *privilege* that other countries lacked and the *oppression* that too many marginalized groups faced. It was symbols of *independence* like the *American flag* juxtaposed against concepts like *mass incarceration*. The students wrestled with the idea of the American dream—a dichotomy of sorts—one defined by traditional success through education and wealth. The other, although relying on wealth as success, acknowledged other, sometimes socially unacceptable avenues.

> ### Note from Anne
>
> So often when students write in school they are asked to name one central thesis and then defend it. However, as Lyschel's students articulated, sometimes more than one conflicting idea can be held simultaneously. How can America be both free and oppressive? Rather than mechanically perform that they know how to support a single point with examples, here writers are using writing to think through ideas. That is, they write individually and collaboratively to complicate and clarify the understandings they had when they first entered the room. This is just one example of how writing is a powerful tool for thinking.

To extend the conversation and provide our first opportunity for analysis, I offered students, who were placed in groups of four, two sets of song lyrics. Using songs as texts was a choice I thought to be nonthreatening and engaging. Students analyzed lyrics with varying perspectives on what it means to be an American by artists like Nas, Lana Del Rey, James Brown, Jay-Z, Rihanna, J. Cole, James Blunt, Carrie Underwood, Kanye West, Toby Keith, Meek Mill, Green Day, and Bambu.

Songs on American Identity

Nas, "America"
Lana Del Rey, "American"
James Brown, "Living in America"
Jay-Z, "American Dreamin'"
Rihanna, "American Oxygen"
J. Cole, "Miss America"
James Blunt, "Miss America"

Carrie Underwood, "All American Girl"
Kanye West, "Made in America"
Toby Keith, "Made in America"
Meek Mill, "Young Black America"
Green Day, "American Idiot"
Bambu, "America"

In writing they answered a set of analysis questions about the central ideas and overlapping or conflicting themes in the lyrics, the songwriters' use of rhetoric—diction and tone—and other devices that impact the message, and how their own views were confirmed or contradicted by the lyrics they read. Students shared how some lyrics paralleled and resonated with their own lives, lyrics like "Comin' from the bottom, it's so hard to make a plan. Know them kids beefin', they let it get out of hand" (Meek Mill). Students discussed similar examples of oppression they too had experienced in their own communities, education, and personal lives.

This was our first introduction to the idea of disrupting texts—a movement to "make space for the rich literary & intellectual history of people of color and other marginalized groups" (Ebarvia, 2018). It's the idea that as educators we can push for inclusivity of diverse voices into our canon; that in the reading of American literature, we are considering various American identities and allowing our writing to rely vastly on personal experiences, including our interactions with reading, and to come from a place of truth. Our goal over the semester was to use writing as a form of inquiry, discovery, and healing—writing about texts and ideas that are complex, intricate, sensitive, and critical and to extend that writing into academic forms and spaces—to use writing as a platform for advocacy and argument. For this to happen, our reading needed to be done from a critical standpoint—confronting social issues and analyzing the roles of speakers, authors, characters, and individuals within our texts. In our readings, we frequently evaluated the progression or stagnation of socially constructed gender, economic, and racial norms. In our writings through fiction, nonfiction, and other creative forms like spoken word, we assessed the impact of these structures on our own lives. Writing became a way of navigating through ideas and the vehicle we used to extend our voices beyond the classroom.

My goal was not only to introduce and write about relevant and current texts, but also to pair classic canonical texts with contemporary pieces. We explored themes from works such as Elizabeth Acevedo's *The Poet X* and Toni Adeyemi's *Children of Blood and Bone*, traversed through the neighborhoods of South Africa with Trevor Noah's *Born a Crime*, and juxtaposed the transcendental ideas of Emerson and Thoreau against Brian Mooney's poem "The Transcendental Gospel of Freddie Gray" (Gray was a victim of police brutality in 2015). With texts like Ta-Nehishi Coates's *Between the World and Me*, we trekked through the hoods of Baltimore and journeyed to Mecca examining the power, impact, and idea of race as a construct. To prepare students to write about the texts, I always genuinely encouraged them to annotate and close read. Reading and writing, they learned, was purely having a conversation—questioning the events, arguing the reasoning, building empathy for characters, laughing at humorous moments, and channeling our indignation or inquiry into powerful responses.

Close Up: Reading and Writing *Between the World and Me*

Our reading of *Between the World and Me*, although assigned as a project, later evolved into a layered and burgeoning dialogue about race, education, violence, and injustice. The conversation grew like intricately designed vines stretching throughout the halls of our building. Students crafted questions to engage with other students, faculty, and staff: *What did Coates mean when he said race is the child of racism, not the father? Do you agree that "in America, it's traditional to destroy the black body?" How much responsibility should schools have in fostering creativity and creating opportunities for authentic learning and conversations about life?* We created an interactive wall outside of our classroom and invited others in the school to explore the artwork and quotes and to leave responses and feedback on the themes and questions we presented. One teacher wrote on the wall about the idea of race as a social construct as argued by scientists and notable authors: "Particularly, the use of race to create a caste system or social stratification among human beings was done so to create and protect systems of power. Race," she argued, "therefore protects a system of power for dominant groups, just as gender and class do." The students now had a larger audience and so, more willingly, embraced the idea of writing as a conversation. They were invested in the text, they felt accountable for their ideas, and they became more willing to defend these ideas in a longer piece of writing.

> **Note from Anne**
>
> As their writing leaves the room and as voices of others enter it, these writers are learning firsthand how "writing is embedded in complex social relationships and their appropriate languages." Their genre-crossing and their interactions with readers and others in their "conversation" help to make clear that while sometimes this literacy conversation includes you, other times it is a conversation about you that your own writing can work to disrupt.

Their culminating assignment was a two-page argumentative response. The prompt required the writers to respond fervently to one of Coates's arguments, argue one of the themes presented in the text, or create and support their own argument. The goal of the writing was not to have students closely follow a prompt, but to use writing as a tool for thinking, to delve deeply into rich conversation with the author, with their audience, and with themselves—reflecting on moments in the text where they felt personally connected, countering or supporting prevailing or subtle claims, or illuminating a sentiment that otherwise might have been unrelatable for some readers.

One such piece was Edna's. Responding to the fear that Coates describes throughout his text, she expounded:

> There is a word for practically every fear. Fear of spiders is arachnophobia . . . fear of heights is acrophobia. . . . There is a word for practically every fear but the fear of

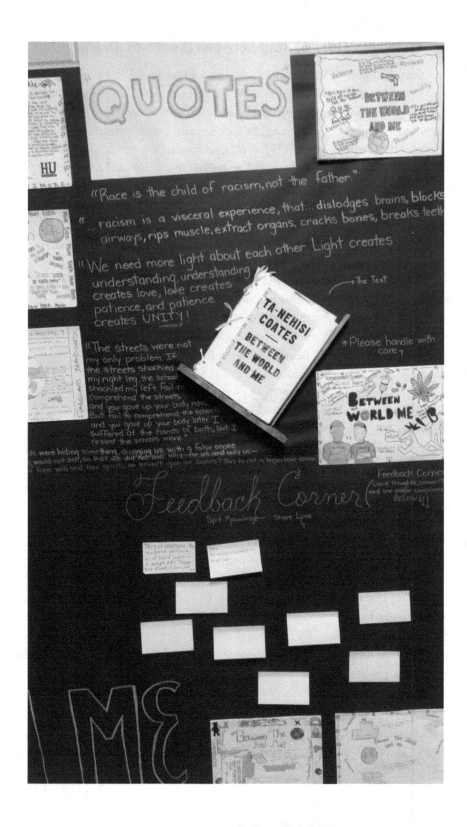

being black and doing black. . . . Black people are constantly dialing our blackness up and down. We are on a teeter-totter of social acceptability. . . . Our fear is not always a screaming dramatic one; it is more of a silent scream—one that we hope someone hears, but no one ever does. It is the sad hopeless, helpless scream of an unfound victim. Our fear is not a gaping wound but more of a slow steady bleeding from a cut on the arm of a hemophiliac. It is steady, unwavering, and it is surely deadly.

Throughout the paper, Edna embedded much of her own experience, balancing this strength and audaciousness of black femininity with a daunting but brash sense of a constant and unwavering fear of being Black:

Our scream is one of shame, changing ourselves, our naturalness to become what should have never existed. It is the mutation of our original selves. . . . That is the kicker about fear—it's crushing. I am not the first to be afraid and I'm certainly not the last.

The fear described in this excerpt is not unfamiliar to many of the students at Central High School and schools like it—in fact, it is one deeply rooted in their everyday experiences. What we discovered through this exploration is that students' writing rises to a new level when they are invited to see writing as a space to express conflicts. Even when solutions seem distant or too complex to approach in a single piece of writing, student writers need opportunities to engage in the conflicts that affect their lives, discuss ways to combat oppressive or unjust systems, and/or engage in various modes of personal catharsis and healing.

In a reflection, Edna later asked other students around the school, "Why is black textual representation important?" Her peers emphasized a yearning for their history, a push away from narratives that heavily focus on strife rather than success, and to see themselves reflected in mainstream and canonical texts. Another student, Zacheriah, examined issues of criminalization, mass incarceration, and the safety of men of color. He posed the question, "Is there a space where Black men can feel safe?"

Zach's question stemmed from his engagement with various texts but also from his own experiences as a Black man: "While I was watching the documentary, *13th*, one scene stuck out to me the most, as a 16 year old black boy watching it with my mother." Zach played for the audience a scene from the film that showed a series of Black men being brutalized by White officers. He spoke about the

Note from Anne

I love how the students have learned from Lyschel to open conversations with questions. When I reflect on the conversations I usually hear or participate in, they tend to begin with statements, not questions. And in so many of our online and political spaces, they seem to begin *and end* with statements—that is, they are not invitations to a conversation at all, representing finalized, closed positions rather than openings for learning or even change. The questions posed by Lyschel's students, in contrast, come not only with knowledge and assumptions on the part of the asker, but also with a desire to learn from and think with others.

rhetorical war on Black lives. . . . Every single one of these people were slandered, their names were dragged . . . and I was 16 when I saw this, I didn't yet know who I was, but I knew my own mortality before I learned my identity. It's hard to know that a 16 year old boy could die and have something from his past demonize his existence. I figured out that it's easier to criminalize someone by dehumanizing their entire existence.

Together, Edna and Zach studied the implications of racial and systemic inequities outside of and within education and proposed ways to dismantle those systems and create a more positive school culture and equitable learning opportunities for all students. They were later able to expand their traditional academic essays into multimodal pieces that included video interviews, panel discussions, and a digital presentation with music and images. Throughout this experience, the process of writing was continually evolving for both students. The traditional essay was neither the beginning nor the end of their writing journeys—a testament to the relationship students build with their writing as they assess its purpose and impact.

Think about what we as adults, educators, and authors want our own writing to accomplish both personally and professionally. Whether it is to teach, inform, or entertain through published or nonpublished works, we are always mindful of our *why*. Rarely do we waste time or take pleasure in meaningless writing. Even in our quietest moments of writing, when we fill our pages with words too private to share, we are intentional—in finding the right words to say and fulfilling whatever desire led us to the page in the first place. Writing in the classroom should be approached from this perspective. The goal should be clearly outlined and authentic. When this happens, the writing may serve a much greater purpose. For example, students composed a conference proposal with their essays in mind. Building on what they had written and on class conversations and the activities I have described here, two students were selected to present at the 2018 Harvard Alumni of Color Conference. To prepare their presentation, they were able to collaborate on themes, strategies, and discussions that were already woven into the fabric of the class community.

Principled Teaching

Woven throughout the teaching I have described here are threads of some core principles, articulated in the Principles document. First, *writing and reading are related*. So often in school we read first, and then we write to prove that we have read or, somewhat better, to build on what we have read. The reading and the writing remain separate, happening at different times in a sequence of instruction. However, in my classes, students constantly move between the writing of others

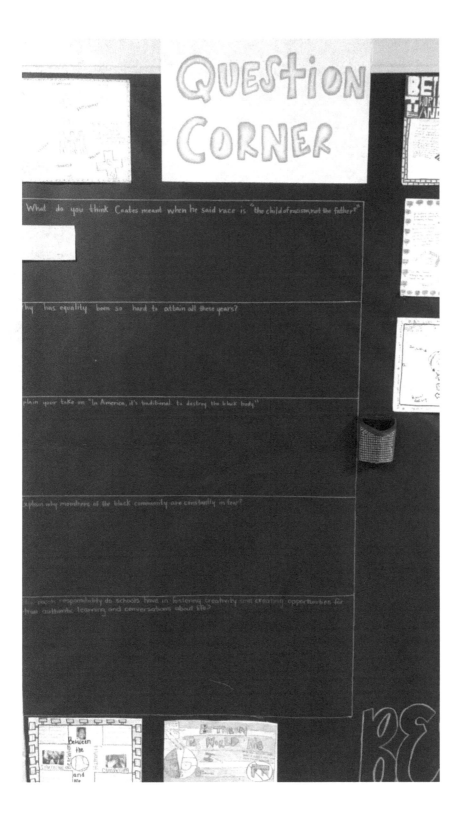

and their own. They quote written texts and one another. They produce texts for audiences not only to read but also to respond to, as in the wall activity described earlier. And on a broader level, when it comes to the complex dynamics of race, oppression, and power in the world in which students are living, they are engaged in both reading and *writing* that world as they seek to disrupt systems of oppression and rewrite better structures. They come to see reading and writing as an extended conversation.

Second, *writing is a tool for thinking*. From written annotations of a text to reflective writing, students write not just to show what they have learned, but also to engage in constant inquiry. In writing, they work through the complexities of texts and issues, and they find stances among the voices of other writers.

Third, and deeply related, is the principle that *writing is embedded in complex social relationships and their appropriate languages*: "In every writing situation, the writer, the reader, and all relevant others live in a structured social order, where some people's words count more than others, where being heard is more difficult for some people than others, where some people's words come true and others' do not" (p. xiii). The students I have described here move across fields of language in which these power relationships are apparent, and they do so moving across spheres of communication from our classroom, to the halls of our school, to a national academic conference. In each of these spaces, they use and further develop resources of the languages and literacies that are effective in those spaces.

I've always argued that writing should feel personal, yet oftentimes students see writing very narrowly—as graded assignments, word counts, formats, and wasted copy paper to be discarded after it's submitted. What we forget to do is celebrate—celebrate the small pieces of writing, the conversations, the artwork, the vulnerable moments, the brave moments, the steps that lead to the final essay. Writing assignments have for so long created inevitable anxieties but never enough thrill, passion, empathy, and other emotions writers experience when they pen their words to a page. Students should learn not only to read but also to write between the lines—each line figuratively mimicking the cardiopulmonary rhythm strip on an EKG. If we celebrate the *life* we get from great writing and discourse, subsequently, feeling affirmed and confident, students will gift you and the world with their best.

Occasions to engage authentically and thoughtfully with texts and with our world, in ways that resonate with students' experiences and voices, should be scrupulous and frequent, like the transition music played throughout the school six times a day for all to hear. The song choice is always intentional. It must be, out of sheer responsibility—whether it is an inspirational staff pick, a holiday-themed ballad, or a student request like Post Malone's "Congratulations" the week before graduation. So, when Andra Day again belts, *"When the silence isn't quiet, and it feels like it's getting hard to breathe . . . ,"* I can't help but think of the students who feel stifled not only by the heaviness of their circumstances *but also* sometimes by the lack of relevance and meaning in what they are tasked to do at school. Reading, writing, and any other practices used to teach or formatively assess should give students voice and allow their voices to vibrate melodiously, loudly, or indignantly throughout the school building and beyond.

Chapter Seven

Contemplating Civic Identity: Explorations through Multimodal Writing

Janelle Quintans Bence

> Composing occurs in different modalities and technologies.

Note from Anne

Janelle Quintans Bence teaches at New Tech High @ Coppell in the suburban Dallas–Fort Worth metroplex. The "rookies" in her ninth-grade English class engage many texts across multiple modes in the course of an inquiry cycle, illustrating the principle that composing occurs in different modalities and technologies. These texts don't simply communicate content for the students to learn; they also inform the students' choices as writers creating culminating multimodal digital stories that communicate new understandings.

I have taught other levels, from tenth through twelfth, but I always return to ninth grade— "rookies," as we call them—at New Tech High at Coppell (NTH@C), a small choice school in an affluent suburb of Dallas. NTH@C is focused on project-based learning (PBL), in which learners work collaboratively to solve real-world problems, integrating technology to help research and demonstrate understanding of possible solutions to authentic tasks. In this chapter, I describe how my students and I worked through issues of civic identity through multimodal writing, in keeping with the principle that "composing occurs in different modalities and technologies." We did this through a series of explorations across print and digital literacies, ranging from Shakespeare, to documentary film, to historical documents, to found poems, to tweets, to multimodal digital stories.

Opening: The Love and Hate We Give

We approached ideas about civic identity through a range of texts and driving questions, beginning with "Why is it important to understand the fine line between love and hate [as the adage says]?" This initial question was broad, messy, and wide open but, most important, provocative and relevant. This inquiry spoke to students' personal values, but also necessitated understanding what these emotions could mean in various contexts beyond just familial or friendly or romantic— extending to broader civic life.

We began with a literary exploration of love and hate by reading and analyzing William Shakespeare's *Romeo and Juliet*. Learners understood that loyalty to family, along with the images and positions of those families in the local scheme of power, drives much of the violence and hateful acts that occur in the play. Through discussion, they also came to see how both love and inter-group hate are as alive in their own relationships and lives as they were in those of the Capulets and Montagues. This literary beginning set the stage to look at similar themes in today's contexts as students came to explore civic identity in the world at large.

Connecting to Historical Voices: Encountering and Tweeting Quotes

Next, we broadened our study of civic identity to move beyond the notion of familial loyalty to include national identity through *American Creed*, a powerful documentary broadcast on PBS in February 2018. The documentary offers six vignettes about people who saw the American dream challenged in their communities and took action to help. The film focuses on snapshots of what engaged citizens look like across the country. *American Creed* poses questions such as "What does it mean to be American?" "Is there anything that connects us despite our diverse backgrounds and beliefs?" "What aspirations does the 'American Creed' espouse,

Note from Anne

As Janelle references later in this chapter, the National Writing Project established and maintains a youth publishing project connected to *American Creed,* including invitations to write and an interactive set of student products. Details are available at https://writingourfuture .nwp.org/americancreed.

It is worth noting how enriching it is for Janelle's teaching to be connected to this wider group of educators engaging similar curricula and placing student writing in dialogue with a shared text. The best advice I ever received as a teacher was "find your people," and this may be even more true with the teaching of writing because it is such an interpersonal activity that we need trusted colleagues with whom to think it through.

and what happens when those promises are not realized?" "What actions can be taken to help grant more equitable access to the American dream?"

Before we jumped into the film, I set up some reading and writing moments to help students be ready to watch, analyze, and appreciate *American Creed.* Why is groundwork like this so important when dealing with complex issues with teens? With the transition to high school, the navigation of new social circles, the tension of losing habits and characteristics of youth toward more mature, "high school" expectations, adolescents are already engaged in their own identity work, and they do so amidst a range of influences and messages about who they are and who they must be. Because of this, and to make the daunting task of unpacking identity more manageable, I try to ground our work on identity in texts that students can refer to and bring into contact with each other.

I invited learners to look at various short historical texts and documents, such as speeches, poems, and essays from historical figures such as Thomas Jefferson and Frederick Douglass. Learners shared words or phrases that really stuck with them from these writings, words that centered on what it means to be American or part of American society (see Figure 7.1).

This exercise using historical texts allowed students to understand the historical significance and gravity of their inquiry. The need to understand the responsibilities and privileges of being a contributing member of a community is as old as the forming of civilized communities. Examining what others say or believe would also ground students as they moved into introspection on their own identities—especially race, gender, and religion. This type of exploration of others first also provides learners with exposure to vocabulary and concepts needed to articulate their own identities.

After providing some historical pieces, I invited learners to search for more contemporary perspectives of what it means to be American or to define the American Creed as they understood it. Students created their own collection of perspectives through a blend of sources suggested by me and sources discovered through their own investigations. After gathering their research on a Google Doc to curate what they found, they then tweeted out images of these quotes along with messages restating the ideas and connecting those ideas to themselves. Choosing the quotes

Historical Perspectives on the American Creed

Below are six examples, from before the end of the Civil War, of how these ideas and principles were articulated. Words that many often refer to when discussing the content of an American Creed are underlined.

1. "We hold these truths to be self-evident, that all men are created <u>equal</u>, that they are endowed by their Creator with certain <u>unalienable Rights</u>, that among these are <u>Life, Liberty and the pursuit of Happiness</u>." —from the Declaration of Independence, July 4, 1776

2. **"We the People** of the United States, in Order to form a more perfect Union, establish <u>Justice</u>, insure domestic Tranquility, provide for the common defence, promote the general Welfare, and secure the Blessings of <u>Liberty</u> to ourselves and our Posterity, do ordain and establish this Constitution for the United States of America." —Preamble to United States Constitution

3. "Equal and exact <u>justice</u> to all . . . of whatever state or persuasion, religious or political . . . should be the creed of our political faith." —from Thomas Jefferson's first inaugural address, March 4, 1801

4. "We hold these truths to be self-evident: that all men and women are created <u>equal</u>." —from the Seneca Falls Declaration of Rights and Sentiments, July 1848

5. "Four score and seven years ago our fathers brought forth on this continent, a new nation, conceived in <u>Liberty</u>, and dedicated to the proposition that all men are created <u>equal</u>." —from Abraham Lincoln's Gettysburg Address, November 19, 1863

6. "We are fighting for unity; unity of idea; unity of sentiment, unity of object, unity of institutions, in which there shall be no North, no South, no East, no West, no black, no white, but solidarity of the nation, making every slave <u>free</u>, and every <u>free</u> man a voter." —from Frederick Douglass, "Our Work Is Not Done," speech at the Annual Meeting of the American Anti-Slavery Society, Philadelphia, Pennsylvania, December 3–4, 1863

Found contemporary quotes of what it means to be American:

Additional readings about the American Creed:

Figure 7.1. Google Doc: Perspectives on the American Creed.

allowed them to better connect with the topic while providing me more insight into what their possible interests were; in turn, tweeting about their findings served as a form of public sharing.

Viewing *American Creed*: From Family to Nation

With this background knowledge in place, it was time to view *American Creed*. I provided students with a graphic organizer to scaffold their understandings and takeaways as they watched the film (see Figure 7.2). For each scene or vignette, learners were asked to record responses to these questions, drawn from the National Writing Project resources at https://writingourfuture.nwp.org/american creed:

- What is your idea of the American Creed?
- How does your family & community history connect to American Creed?
- How is the American Creed expressed in words, symbols, and rituals?
- How do diverse Americans understand the American Creed?
- How can we express the American Creed through action?
- What do you want to remember?

The graphic organizer helped to support students in attending to these questions as they viewed particular segments of the film.

These questions helped learners focus on the relationship between being a citizen or active member of American society and the need to connect to others. More specifically, each story is about someone who believed very strongly in characteristics of an engaged citizen, such as education, respect for diversity, service, or equity, as well as how each individual does something to live out these aspirations. These questions are also included in the National Writing Project's invitation on their Writing Our Future site, where youth can publish media that responds to these inquiries and to the documentary.

Note from Anne

Access to the film as well as to a set of related educational resources can be found at https://www.americancreed.org/.

Found Poems: Writing Our Stories

Although the film showcases a wide range of stories, there was still a messy open-endedness to this inquiry. Learners needed to reflect on what being American meant to them on a personal level. As they continued to grapple and make sense of America's aspirations and their own roles within these promises, I invited learners to create their first text representing their individual views on what it means to be American.

Learner Name:_____ Section: _____ Date:_____ 1

Scaffolded Notes for American Creed Viewing

Scene	What is your idea of the American Creed?	How does your family & community history connect to American Creed?	How is the American Creed expressed in words, symbols, and rituals?	How do diverse Americans understand the American Creed?	How can we express the American Creed through action?	What do you want to remember?
Introduction Rice and Kennedy						Challenge faced: Actions taken as Possible Solutions:
Pennsylvania Joe Maddon 5:01						Challenge faced: Actions taken as Possible Solutions:

Learner Name:_____ Section: _____ Date:_____ 2

Scaffolded Notes for American Creed Viewing

Scene	What is your idea of the American Creed?	How does your family & community history connect to American Creed?	How is the American Creed expressed in words, symbols, and rituals?	How do diverse Americans understand the American Creed?	How can we express the American Creed through action?	What do you want to remember?
David Kennedy 13:54						Challenge faced: Actions taken as Possible Solutions:
Tulsa, OK Deidre Prevett 18:21						Challenge faced: Actions taken as Possible Solutions:

Learner Name:_____ Section: _____ Date:_____ 3

Scaffolded Notes for American Creed Viewing

Scene	What is your idea of the American Creed?	How does your family & community history connect to American Creed?	How is the American Creed expressed in words, symbols, and rituals?	How do diverse Americans understand the American Creed?	How can we express the American Creed through action?	What do you want to remember?
Condoleezza Rice 24:45						Challenge faced: Actions taken as Possible Solutions:
Central New Jersey Junot Diaz 32:44						Challenge faced: Actions taken as Possible Solutions:

Figure 7.2. Multipage form for taking scaffolded notes while viewing *American Creed*.

Figure 7.2. Continued.

Learner Name:_____   Section: _____   Date:_____   4

Scaffolded Notes for American Creed Viewing

Scene	What is your idea of the American Creed?	How does your family & community history connect to American Creed?	How is the American Creed expressed in words, symbols, and rituals?	How do diverse Americans un-derstand the American Creed?	How can we express the American Creed through action?	What do you want to remember?
Milwaukee, Wisconsin Tegan Griffith 41:07						Challenge faced: Actions taken as Possible Solutions:
Seattle, Wash-ington Eric Liu 50:05						Challenge faced: Actions taken as Possible Solutions:

Learner Name:_____   Section: _____   Date:_____   5

Scaffolded Notes for American Creed Viewing

Scene	What is your idea of the American Creed?	How does your family & community history connect to American Creed?	How is the American Creed expressed in words, symbols, and rituals?	How do diverse Americans un-derstand the American Creed?	How can we express the American Creed through action?	What do you want to remember?
Berkeley, California Mark Meckler and Joan Blades 57:47						Challenge faced: Actions taken as Possible Solutions:
Dumas, Arkansas Terrence Davenport and Leila Janah 1:09:05						Challenge faced: Actions taken as Possible Solutions:

Learner Name:_____   Section: _____   Date:_____   6

Scaffolded Notes for American Creed Viewing

Scene	What is your idea of the American Creed?	How does your family & community history connect to American Creed?	How is the American Creed expressed in words, symbols, and rituals?	How do diverse Americans un-derstand the American Creed?	How can we express the American Creed through action?	What do you want to remember?
Discussions with Students at Stanford						Challenge faced: Actions taken as Possible Solutions:

Yes, this is a daunting task for anyone. Through my efforts to provide models and other viewpoints and experiences of others articulating their ideas of engaged citizens, I hoped learners would find support for making their own meaning. To do this, I suggested more poems, documents, and articles for learners to use (see Figure 7.3).

As they explored texts like these, students captured words and phrases that we call "hot spots" in their reading. These are attention grabbers, ideas that stuck with my students. On a shared Google Doc, they recorded the source, the hot spot, and why it spoke to them. They then used these borrowed words to create their own found poems about being engaged in American society. The questions to be explored in their found poems were:

- What is it that I value as being an American or someone who is part of American society?

- What has influenced what I value and what makes those priorities "American"?

- What stories impacted what I consider to be American?

- Are these values abstract ideas or actions?

- What impact does understanding one's cultural identity have on the rest of who I am as a person?

Learners also collected images that supported these concepts. (See one learner's completed Found Words and Symbols Doc in Figure 7.4.) Figure 7.5 shows student Isabella's found poem.

Making Multimodal Digital Stories

The final project of the unit was to make digital stories that included narration of students' found poems and images of their found or created symbols (see Figure 7.6). In creating products that cross modes and blend them, writers have opportunities to think more deeply about both the modes of communication they choose and the content they are communicating. Some modes, they find, are more suited to particular content than others; different modes may foreground different aspects of the same ideas.

Students gave one another feedback at least three times in the process: for the first draft of the poem, for the recorded narration, and for a draft of the complete

Note from Anne

Viewing a video text with enough attention to be able to have a deep analytical conversation afterward is tough. Janelle works to scaffold viewing and note-taking for her students, both with questions and with a handout meant to shape their notes in response to those questions. I have also found it necessary to stop videos frequently, giving students time to record their noticings, and also time to talk about their understandings so far and their expectations and questions going forward. At one time, I saw films as "faster" texts than print for students to work with; now I think the opposite. Given the prevalence of video in today's reading material, I am heartened to know there are teachers like Janelle helping students write in response to video.

- Rice, C. (2017, June 8). America's second democratic opening. Retrieved October 28, 2019, from Medium website: https://medium.com/freeman-spogli-institute-for-international-studies/americas-second-democratic-opening-d790c6356151
- "Let America Be America Again" by Langston Hughes (available at poets.org)
- "America" by Walt Whitman
- "Letter from a Birmingham Jail" by Martin Luther King, Jr. (Available at https://kinginstitute.stanford.edu/king-papers/documents/letter-birmingham-jail, including a scan of the original document as well as audio of King reading it later)
- Healy, J., Bidgood, J., & Blinder, A. (2017, July 3). A patriotic Fourth: What does that mean now? *The New York Times.* Retrieved from https://www.nytimes.com/2017/07/03/us/july-fourth-patriotism.html
- "America" by Claude McKay (Available at poets.org)
- United Nations. (1948). Universal declaration of human rights. Retrieved October 28, 2019, from https://www.un.org/en/about-us/universal-declaration-of-human-rights

Figure 7.3. Supplemental readings.

narrated digital story. Giving and receiving feedback guided learners to remix their makes for greater effectiveness, but it also helped them to be more critical of media as a whole by reading and viewing the digital stories more closely and examining them through the rubric's lens (see Appendix A at the end of this chapter).

Students' digital stories, once complete, were posted on YouTube. You can view a sample of these at these links:

The Patriot by Isabella Zeff https://youtu.be/otjnYK-4NTY

Fresh Start by Annie Brandenburg https://youtu.be/AkIYsh2yKUk

Immigrant by Sahil Chiniwala https://youtu.be/AkIYsh2yKUk

Note from Anne

When writers provide one another with feedback, the feedback helps them to improve their products. But collaborating to provide feedback also builds relationships between members of the writing community. Further, it helps them to form a shared group value of seeing writing as an iterative process. (See the principle "Writing is a process" on pp. xix–xxi.)

While the digital stories these learners created vary in form and content, they share some common characteristics. First, all required that students make thoughtful decisions about what to include, how to sequence materials, and how to pace or time them for most effective communication with their intended audience. Further, all involved expressions of identity along with ideas about American citizenship and/or society.

Finally, the learners reflected on their work in the form of tweets (Figure 7.7). Using tweets has several rationales: First, they are a familiar genre to these learners. Second, tweets are already commonly used to communicate ideas connected to politics and activism. Third, the brevity of tweets challenges the students to think deeply about what they wish to convey, in the most precise and concise terms possible.

Cited Source (name, author, or URL)	Found Hotspot or Image	Theme or Value	Why did you choose it?
Preamble to the UDHR (Universal Declaration of Human Rights)	"Whereas recognition of the inherent dignity and of the equal and inalienable rights of all members of the human family is the foundation of freedom, justice and peace in the world,"	Because this is mentioning similar things to the preamble of the constitution (inalienable rights).	Because the values while global, still match up to the American Creed.
UDHR Article 3	"Everyone has the right to life, liberty and security of person."	Similar to the American Right to life, liberty and pursuit of happiness.	Because when people think of American values this is often what comes to mind first and so it is what is important.
https://obamawhite house.archives.gov/blog/2016/11/30/president-obamas-top-ten-actions-accelerate-american-entrepreneurship	[Image of President Obama from 2014, meeting African American entrepreneurs at the White House]	Because this shows Americans acceptance and tolerance to other races	I chose it because with our new president and his comments it seems as if this American value is disappearing.
https://www.panini.com/it/node/923		While this image doesn't directly look at americans you can link it to the American values because we value efficiency	I chose this one because it is an american value that can be interpreted both positively and negatively.

Figure 7.4. Excerpt from one learner's Found Words and Symbols Doc.

The Patriot

"From dark Ireland's shore,
And Poland's plain, and England's grassy lea,
And from Black Africa's strand they came
To build a 'homeland of the free.'"

A patchwork patterned quilt
Stitched together end to end
Or strange pieces chopped
From different trees they've stemmed
Built, cobbled, nailed as one
Into a grand ship of legend

Her sails of liberty blow
Her freedom flag waves with pride
Cannons of justice pierce her hull
Patriot reads the proud writing on her side

People come from all around
To join her motley crew
Of liberty and unity
For freedom and for life anew

All the boats that sail these seven seas
The *Patriot* will eclipse
A beautiful "nation of nations"
A magnificent ship of ships

Though from many different places
Both far away and near
Once aboard the mighty ship
Each member may speak with no fear

From her crow's nest on her mast
To the rooms beneath her decks
Every inch of ship is equal
That each of them do protect

The *Patriot* sails through swirling waters
The captain's charting never errs
He spins the wheel and steers the ship
But plots a course to nowhere

"For all the dreams they've dreamed
And all the songs they've sung

And all the hopes they've held
And all the flags" they've flung

The *Patriot* is stagnant
All is not what it seems
This ship is going nowhere
This ship of righteous dreams

A tiny fatal flaw
Lay hidden in the plans
To build the ship of freedom
Overlooked by many hands

There's but a tiny crack
Splitting down her side
So the crew may talk of glorious dreams
But may never turn the tide

Just one person on the boat
Sees the water seeping in
They rally the crew to action
To restore her from within

The water's gone and in its place
Understanding trickles in
Of their place and role and part
To which ignorant they've been

Their talk is well and good
Ideas never fail
But the ship must sail to somewhere
Or it is all to no avail

Now the captain charts a course
The *Patriot* sails across the ocean blue
With equality not just of their own
But for the whole world too

"From dark Ireland's shore,
And Poland's plain, and England's grassy lea,
And from Black Africa's strand they came
To build a 'homeland of the free.'"

Figure 7.5. Found poem by Isabella.

American Identity: Found Symbols and Words Digital Story

What we read, watch, listen to, grow up around shapes our identity.

In this activity, we will explore just one segment of who you are: your American Identity.

Consider the following questions:

- What is it that I value as being an American or someone who is part of American society?
- What has influenced what I value and what makes those priorities "American"?
- What stories impacted what I consider to be American?
- Are these values abstract ideas or actions?
- What impact does understanding one's cultural identity have on the rest of who I am as a person?

You have begun collecting various quotes about what others believe to be part of the American Creed. In your **PERSONAL** Perspectives on the American Creed Document (it should be in the American Creed folder I asked you to create), add the bottom links from this *Perspectives of the American Creed* doc.

Read the documents.

Create a new Google Doc using this Found Words and Symbols. Copy and paste "Hot Spots" from the readings. Please make certain to cite the source.

Also add images into your table. Make certain to complete the ENTIRE table.

With this table, you will create a digital story with a narration of your "Found Poem."

Criteria:

- Poem narration is a minimum of 2 minutes, maximum 3 minutes.
- Images must be high res—NOT pixelated.
- Only use images that are licensed for reuse.
- You may add your own words to your poem.
- Your poem should respond to the above questions.
- You may use iMovie Premier Pro.
- Narration must be clear and good sound quality.
- Include a citation screen at the end of your Digital Story.
- You must have a draft for class, Tuesday, January 23, 2018. Be ready to give and receive feedback.

Use this RUBRIC to guide your work.

Figure 7.6. Assignment for making multimodal stories about American identity.

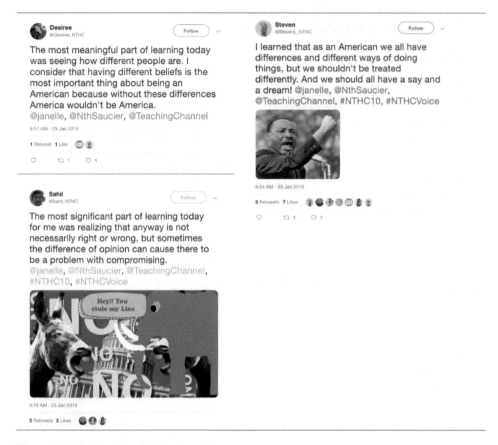

Figure 7.7. Students' reflective tweets.

Making Media: Multiple Sources, Multiple Identities, Multiple Literacies

Being an engaged citizen is about identifying our ideals and aspirations and working toward those for ourselves and others, even while knowing that other perspectives exist as we ultimately move toward common ground, respect, and understanding. The various single-mode and multimodal expressions of civic identity that these learners made, such as digital stories, found poems, and tweets, allowed learners to develop and share ideas of what they valued, as well as what they sought to change or improve to get closer to that elusive American dream. Students' learning wouldn't have been as deep or effective by writing just a research paper or an expository essay or poem; making a multimedia piece leveraged students' messages in a medium more appealing to others and more in keeping with the media they themselves read and view outside of school. It's one thing to know what you want to communicate. It's quite another to know how to communicate it effectively.

Our Media, Ourselves: Writing as a Social and Civic Practice

This work connects most directly to the principle that composing happens in different modalities and technologies. While composing in school settings has historically privileged print to the exclusion of other ways of composing, the Principles document makes the point that even print is multimodal, using not only letters and words but also space, language, layout, and of course images such as figures and tables within texts. As the position statement explains, "As technologies for composing have expanded, 'composing' has increasingly referred to a suite of activities in varied modalities. Composers today work with many modalities, including language, layout, still images, other visuals, video, and sound" (p. xiv). If writing instruction is to support writers in the contexts they encounter in life outside the classroom, then they need classroom instruction that encompasses these multiple modalities and the composing processes associated with them.

As with any identity work, creating digital stories that explore civic identity is a complex task for student writers. This very personal and authentic call to "make" requires careful scaffolding with moments to write and read and work both independently and collaboratively. My learners understood the need to read extensively for information and vocabulary that helped to clarify their ideas. They wrote to capture values that resonated with them and were part of their own civic identities, but this work also helped to establish a mutual understanding of terms from one student to another. My learners relied on one another throughout their writing for feedback to refine again and again. Though their texts (and especially their digital stories shared on YouTube) were primarily intended for readers outside the classroom, sharing their texts with one another during and after their composition also gave our classroom community a better idea of who each of us was in this particular context. This type of civic learning engages my students in thinking beyond the classroom and how their learning situates itself in their lives. The authentic application of literacy skills, coupled with helping learners explore their identities, makes for a winning combination. The intersection of identity work and multimodal literacy breathes life and excitement into my teaching.

Appendix A: Rubric

NTH@C

2017 Critical Literacies Rubric: American Creed Found Poem*

Learner Name: _____
Evaluator: _____ DATE: _____

Knowledge & Thinking

	EMERGING	DEVELOPING	PROFICIENT 10th Grade Ready	ADVANCED 10th Grade Level
ELA Content	(1) Reading/Vocabulary Development. Students do not understand new vocabulary and do not use it when reading and writing. Students are expected to: (C) do not attempt to produce analogies that describe a function of an object or its description; (3) Reading/Comprehension of Literary Text/Poetry. Students do not understand, do not try to make inferences or draw conclusions about the structure and elements of poetry and do not provide evidence from text to support their understanding. Students do not attempt to analyze the effects of diction and imagery (e.g., controlling images, figurative language, understatement, overstatement, irony, paradox) in poetry. (8) Reading/Comprehension of Informational Text/Culture and History. Students do not analyze, make inferences or draw conclusions about the author's purpose in cultural, historical, and contemporary contexts and do not provide evidence from the text to support their understanding.	(1) Reading/Vocabulary Development. Students somewhat understand new vocabulary and try to use it when reading and writing. Students are expected to: (C) attempt to produce analogies that describe a function of an object or its description; (3) Reading/Comprehension of Literary Text/Poetry. Students somewhat understand, try to make inferences and draw conclusions about the structure and elements of poetry and try to provide evidence from text to support their understanding. Students attempt to analyze the effects of diction and imagery (e.g., controlling images, figurative language, understatement, overstatement, irony, paradox) in poetry. (8) Reading/Comprehension of Informational Text/Culture and History. Students attempt to analyze, make inferences and draw conclusions about the author's purpose in cultural, historical, and contemporary contexts and provide evidence from the text to support their understanding.	(1) Reading/Vocabulary Development. Students understand new vocabulary and use it when reading and writing. Students are expected to: (C) produce analogies that describe a function of an object or its description; (3) Reading/Comprehension of Literary Text/Poetry. Students understand, make inferences and draw conclusions about the structure and elements of poetry and provide evidence from text to support their understanding. Students are expected to analyze the effects of diction and imagery (e.g., controlling images, figurative language, understatement, overstatement, irony, paradox) in poetry. (8) Reading/Comprehension of Informational Text/Culture and History. Students analyze, make inferences and draw conclusions about the author's purpose in *cultural, historical, and contemporary contexts and provide evidence from the text to support their understanding.*	(1) Reading/Vocabulary Development. Students easily understand new vocabulary and use it effectively when reading and writing. Students are expected to: (C) produce highly effective analogies that describe a function of an object or its description; (3) Reading/Comprehension of Literary Text/Poetry. Students understand, make inferences and draw conclusions about the structure and elements of poetry and provide evidence from text to support their understanding. Students are expected to easily analyze the effects of diction and imagery (e.g., controlling images, figurative language, understatement, overstatement, irony, paradox) in poetry. (8) Reading/Comprehension of Informational Text/Culture and History. Students analyze, make inferences and draw conclusions about the author's purpose in cultural, historical, and contemporary contexts and provide evidence from the text to support their understanding.

0............4	5............6	7............8	9............10
ARGUMENT *What is the evidence that the student can develop an argument?*			
Poem demonstrates little awareness of the following questions (responses may be explicitly or implicitly):	Poem demonstrates some reflection of the following questions (responses may be explicitly or implicitly):	Poem demonstrates reflection of the following questions (responses may be explicitly or implicitly):	Poem demonstrates deep reflection and understanding significance of the following questions (responses may be explicitly or implicitly):
• What is it that I value as being an American or someone who is part of American Society? • What has influenced what I value and what makes those priorities "American"? • What stories impacted what I consider to be American? • Are these values abstract ideas or actions? • What impact does understanding one's cultural identity have on the rest of who I am as a person?	• What is it that I value as being an American or someone who is part of American Society? • What has influenced what I value and what makes those priorities "American"? • What stories impacted what I consider to be American? • Are these values abstract ideas or actions? • What impact does understanding one's cultural identity have on the rest of who I am as a person?	• What is it that I value as being an American or someone who is part of American Society? • What has influenced what I value and what makes those priorities "American"? • What stories impacted what I consider to be American? • Are these values abstract ideas or actions? • What impact does understanding one's cultural identity have on the rest of who I am as a person?	• What is it that I value as being an American or someone who is part of American Society? • What has influenced what I value and what makes those priorities "American"? • What stories impacted what I consider to be American? • Are these values abstract ideas or actions? • What impact does understanding one's cultural identity have on the rest of who I am as a person?
0............4	5............6	7............8	9............10

Written Communication

	EMERGING	DEVELOPING	PROFICIENT	ADVANCED
LANGUAGE AND CONVENTIONS *What is the evidence that the learner can use language skillfully to communicate ideas?*	• Language, style, and tone are inappropriate to the purpose and audience* • Attempts to follow the norms and conventions of writing in the discipline/genre with major, consistent errors**	• Language, style, and tone are mostly appropriate to the purpose and audience with some lapses* • Follows the norms and conventions of writing in the discipline/genre with some errors** • Has errors in grammar, usage, and mechanics that	• Language, style, and tone are appropriate to the purpose and audience with minor lapses* • Follows the norms and conventions of writing in the discipline/genre with minor errors** • Has some minor errors in grammar, usage, and	• Language, style, and tone are appropriate to the purpose and audience* • Follows the norms and conventions of writing in the discipline/genre** • Is generally free of distracting errors in

	0 4	5 6	7 8	9 10
	• Has an accumulation of errors in grammar, usage, and mechanics that distract from or interfere with meaning • When appropriate for the task, textual citation is missing or incorrect • Your hot spots were not well organized. • Your poem did not respond to the questions Author's Craft: • uses one or no literary devices • literary devices detract from author's purpose • Title screen absent	distract from or interfere with meaning • When appropriate for the task, cites textual evidence partially or using incorrect format • You did not add your own words to your poem. • Your poem responded to the most of the questions Author's Craft: • uses less than 3 literary devices • literary devices do not support author's purpose • devices use may seem a bit forced at times • Title Screen missing an element	mechanics that do not distract from or interfere with meaning • When appropriate for the task, cites textual evidence with some minor errors • You added your own words to your poem. • Your poem should respond to the questions. Author's Craft: • **uses at least 3 literary devices** • literary devices support author's purpose • devices are used seamlessly and feel natural rather than forced • Title Screen with title of poem and learner's name	grammar, usage, and mechanics • When appropriate for the task, cites textual evidence consistently and accurately • You wrote with mostly your own words to your poem. • Your poem artfully responded to the questions Author's Craft: • uses **more than** 3 literary devices • literary devices achieve author's purpose • effectively uses extended metaphor in a non-distracting way • devices are used creatively, poets take ownership and pride in using them • Title Screen with title of poem and learner's name

Writing Process
What is the evidence that the learner can engage in the writing process to produce polished texts?
	• Demonstrates little to no effort to use the writing process:
	  o does not generate ideas and does not gather information relevant to the topic and purpose, using no outside sources
	  o does not conference in order to evaluate relevance, quality, sufficiency, and depth
		• Demonstrates effort to use the writing process:
		  o generates few ideas and gathers little information relevant to the topic and purpose, using but not recording outside sources
		  o conferences but does not evaluate relevance, quality, sufficiency, and depth of preliminary ideas and information, organize material generated, and formulate a
			• Consistently uses the writing process:
			  o generate ideas and gather information relevant to the topic and purpose, using and showing attempts to keep records of outside sources
			  o conferences in order to evaluate relevance, quality, sufficiency, and depth of preliminary ideas and information, organize material generated, and formulate a
				• Effectively uses the writing process:
				  o generates several ideas and gathers much information relevant to the topic and purpose, keeping careful records of outside sources
				  o avidly seeks conferencing opportunities in order to evaluate relevance,

	0............4 (EMERGING)	5............6 (DEVELOPING)	7............8 (PROFICIENT)	9............10 (ADVANCED)
	of preliminary ideas and information, organize material generated, and formulate a thesis ○ Recognize the importance of revision as the key to effective writing. Each draft shows no refinement key ideas and organize them more logically and fluidly, use language more precisely and effectively, and draw the reader to the author's purpose ○ Does not edit writing for proper voice, tense, and syntax, assuring that it conforms to standard English.	thesis. ○ Recognize the importance of revision as the key to effective writing. Each draft shows little refinement key ideas and organize them more logically and fluidly, use language more precisely and effectively, and draw the reader to the author's purpose ○ Edits writing for proper voice, tense, and syntax, assuring that it conforms to standard English, when appropriate with pervasive errors.	thesis. ○ Recognizes the importance of revision as the key to effective writing. Each draft shows refinement key ideas and organize them more logically and fluidly, use language more precisely and effectively, and draw the reader to the author's purpose ○ Edits writing for proper voice, tense, and syntax, assuring that it conforms to standard English, when appropriate with minor lapses.	quality, sufficiency, depth of preliminary ideas and information, organize material generated, and formulate a thesis ○ Recognizes the importance of revision as the key to effective writing. Each draft shows developed refinement of key ideas and organizes them more logically and fluidly, use language more precisely and effectively, and draw the reader to the author's purpose ○ Edits writing for proper voice, tense, syntax, assuring that it conforms to standard English with few errors that hinder meaning.
	0............4	5............6	7............8	9............10

Oral Communication

	EMERGING	DEVELOPING	PROFICIENT College Ready	ADVANCED College Level
USE OF DIGITAL MEDIA / VISUAL DISPLAYS *What is the evidence that the learner can use digital media/visual displays to engage and support audience understanding?*	• Digital media or visual displays are confusing, extraneous, or distracting • Poem and slide show ended at different times. • Visuals detracted from performance • Video timings were not used	• Digital media or visual displays are informative and relevant • Little attention to timing • Visuals did little to support meaning of poem • Video timings were ineffective or incorrect	• Digital media or visual displays are appealing, informative, and support audience engagement and understanding • Video timing coincides with ending of performance	• Digital media or visual displays are polished, informative, and support audience engagement and understanding • Video timing is orchestrated to support meaning of the poem
	0............4	5............6	7............8	9............10

PRESENTATION SKILLS *What is the evidence that the learner can control and use appropriate body language and speaking skills to support audience engagement?*	0........4	5........6	7........8	9........10
	• Demonstrates a command of some aspects of presentation skills, including control of body posture and gestures, language fluency, eye contact, clear and audible voice, and appropriate pacing • Presenter's energy, and/or affect are usually appropriate for the audience and purpose of the presentation, with minor lapses • Reads directly from notes or presentation • Audience nor performers are clear on the connection to the American Creed • Images are pixelated. • Images are not licensed for reuse. • PhotoShop Mask image not included. • You did not use iMovie or Premier Pro • Narration isn't of good sound quality. • Does not include a partial citation screen at the end of your Digital Story. • Font used on title screen and elsewhere is not appropriate for context, appealing, or easy to read	• Demonstrates a command of some aspects of presentation skills, including control of body posture and gestures, language fluency, eye contact, clear and audible voice, and appropriate pacing • Presenter's energy, and/or affect are usually appropriate for the audience and purpose of the presentation, with minor lapses • Reads directly from notes or presentation • Audience is disconnected and/or unaware of the connection to American Creed • Images are pixelated • Images are not licensed for reuse. • PhotoShop Mask image not included. • You did not use iMovie or Premier Pro • Narration isn't of good sound quality. • Include a partial citation screen at the end of your Digital Story. • Font used on title screen and elsewhere is somewhat appropriate for context, appealing, and easy to read	• Demonstrates a command of presentation skills, including control of body posture and gestures, eye contact, clear and audible voice, and appropriate pacing • Presenter's energy and affect are appropriate for the audience and support engagement • Images must be high res—NOT pixelated • Only use images that are licensed for reuse. • One of the images is your PhotoShop Mask image. • You may use iMovie Premier Pro. • Narration must be clear and good sound quality. • Include a citation screen at the end of your Digital Story. • Font used on title screen and elsewhere is appropriate for context, appealing, and easy to read	• Demonstrates consistent command of presentation skills, including control of body posture & gestures, eye contact, clear audible voice, & appropriate pacing in a way that keeps the audience engaged • Presenter maintains a presence & a captivating energy that is appropriate to the audience and purpose of the presentation • Presentation is clearly rehearsed and confidently presented • Audience is compelled by the link to the American Creed • Images must be high res— NOT pixelated • Only use images that are licensed for reuse. Also, used original images • One of the images is your PhotoShop Mask image. • You may use iMovie Premier Pro. • Narration is clear and good sound quality. • Includes citation rolling credits at the end of your Digital Story. • Font used on title screen and elsewhere is adds to professional presentation

Agency

	EMERGING	DEVELOPING	PROFICIENT College Ready	ADVANCED College Level
Meet Benchmarks	• Completes few benchmarks and class assignments (poem drafts, Culture Region Slide show, performance auditions, workshops, etc.) and may resist or struggle to use resources and supports • Composes a found poem video that is less than 2 minutes in length (with superfluous pauses)	• Completes some benchmarks and class assignments (poem drafts, rhetorical device workshops, gaining feedback, performance auditions, etc.); and, only when forced to, or at the last minute, uses resources and supports • Composes a found poem video that is less than 2 minutes in length (without superfluous pauses)	• Completes polished benchmarks and class assignments (poem drafts, rhetorical device workshops, gaining feedback, performance auditions, etc.) by using resources and supports when necessary on time. • Composes a found poem video that is at least 2 minutes in length but no more than 3 minutes (without superfluous pauses)	• Achieves personal best work on almost all benchmarks and class assignments (poem drafts, rhetorical device workshops, gaining feedback, performance auditions, etc.) by setting goals, monitoring progress, and using resources and supports • Composes a found poem video more than 2 minutes in length but less than 3 minutes (without superfluous pauses)
	0..............4	5..............6	7..............8	9..............10
Actively Participate	• Stays focused for part of the activity of writing the found poem and recording. During project time often cannot resist distraction or does not notice when or why a loss of focus	• Mostly stays focused on the activity of writing the found poem and recording. During project time knows when and why disengagement or distraction happens	• Actively participates in the activity of writing the found poem and recording. During independent time has strategies for staying focused and resisting most distraction.	• Actively participates and takes initiative on the activity of writing the poem, recording, and independent time and has personal strategies for staying focused
	0..............4	5..............6	7..............8	9..............10

*Rubric reprinted verbatim from docs.google.com/document/d/1S4xNQYr6blLD7rKJTXaV0yvLC9pq7ac229zyo6NcST3Q/edit.

Modified from New Tech Network by New Tech High @ Coppell, November 2016

**Chapter
Eight**

Revision Plans: Teaching Students to Process Their Choices during Interludes for Reflection

Derek Miller

Writing is a process.

Note from Anne

We teachers can say to writers that "writing is a process," and we might even have it posted on a classroom wall or codified in an official curriculum resource. Yet so many student writers seem to prefer a "one and done" way of working, in which first drafts are immediately submitted and promptly forgotten about. In this chapter, Derek Miller shows us how he has provoked thoughtful revision by opening up "interludes" in which his students at Michigan's Royal Oak High School reflect on their work and make concrete "revision plans."

It was March. We were approaching spring break and the time of year when I have to find more and more creative ways to engage my students. Outside my classroom, the Michigan winter had begun to soften toward gray skies and slush. Inside my classroom, I was looking for signs that my previous months of teaching would become visible as growth.

Nick was writing about space trash. In this revision of an argument assignment, I hoped my students would show me that they understood how to explore a piece of evidence by developing their reasoning in ways that would connect to the concerns of readers with a variety of perspectives or whose priorities might vary in terms of the essential issues related to the topic, which was, in this case, space trash. But, in a one-on-one conference with Nick, I could see that he had done little of this.

I pointed this out to him and asked him what his thoughts were about the strategies I had taught to connect evidence to issues and to consider a variety of perspectives.

"I guess I didn't understand," he said.

What to do with a student like Nick? In this chapter, I describe the role that written revision plans have come to play in my classroom. As a teacher, I know that my job is to make my students independent. I want them to be able to do on their own the things I teach them. NCTE's *Professional Knowledge for the Teaching of Writing* statement reminds me of the principle that writing is a process. As process, writing involves thinking moves that writers make over the course of crafting a text. Revision is a critical part of this process, yet it is difficult to manage—for both student writers and teachers. Thinking moves by nature are generally invisible to emerging writers, and by the time they have worked to complete an entire draft, they feel as though they have invested enough of themselves in the product and their thinking has moved on.

I cannot anticipate all of the tasks and purposes each one of my students will need to take up and succeed at throughout their writing lives. Given the time constraints of our school year and the limitations of our curriculum, there are only so many products we can create together. Even if it were in their best interest to somehow move quickly through dozens of different genres and purposes, at best my students would receive only a taste of understanding of each one. Teaching them that writing is a process means that the weight of the instruction falls on es-

Note from Anne

If we view writing as a process, it can be tempting to teach "the process" in a way that suggests it is always the same, or that it is the same for all writers in every writing situation. I hear in Derek Miller's account a reminder that it would probably best be called "writing processes." That is, there are many different processes we might use along the way to completing a piece of writing, and they vary according to writer, situation, purpose, etc. Teaching a writer one process helps them through exactly one piece of writing. Teaching processes, on the other hand, can equip writers to select among a broad range of potential decisions as they write.

sential skills and strategies writers use to understand and make effective writing in many genres and for multiple purposes. When I teach students about the process of revision, what I teach them how to do is to be purposeful about the choices they make.

One part of the content that I teach is about elements of effective writing. However, the skills and strategies writers might use to craft those elements within a draft constitute another step. Further, of equal importance is my focus on "the development of reflective abilities and meta-awareness about writing" (the Principles, p. xix). Alongside their writing, my students must learn to *think* about writing. To help them achieve this, I immerse my students in the process of the craft by teaching them to reflect on and articulate their choices. At multiple points throughout the course of drafting any given text, we have instructional "interludes." My students stop their work, we review it, and—sometimes with and sometimes without instruction—they step aside to write reflections on their choices and create plans for revising the pieces they are working on.

Making Explicit Revision Plans

My students' problems with understanding revision became apparent to me early in my teaching career, and for a long time I had very little idea what to do about them. When I would confer one on one with student writers, the conversations might have been laughable except for the depth of uncertainty, misunderstanding, and miscommunication they seemed to reveal. In a unit on personal narrative, an early revision lesson might focus on using sensory images to evoke the mood of the scene. In a follow-up conference, I might ask a student what they had changed about a passage, and I quickly learned not to be surprised by answers ranging from "I decided to add a story" to "I added more details about my topic" to "I fixed the spelling and took out some of the extra commas I had in there by mistake." Any of these answers might name acceptable changes to a piece of writing, but I also learned to be even less surprised when, after asking a student to point out the changes in the draft, neither they nor I could spot them. Because of conversations like these, I (along with my colleagues) created checklists and quantified specific moves we wished students to make in revision (e.g., students should include three instances of dialogue or twenty sensory images).

The trouble with this "checklist" solution for my writing instruction is that it didn't truly address the problem. Grading every student on whether they have included twenty sensory images in a personal narrative does not tell me whether students understand how and when to use language to evoke a mood in a way that resonates with and supports their purpose. Furthermore, it wasn't clear to me that the solution even produced better writing. The student who struggles to explore the impact of a negative, overbearing soccer coach on her ability as a player, and works to connect the loss of confidence on the field to increased anxiety in school and problems relating to friends, is not less of a writer than the student who paints a vivid detailed picture of the day her team won the championship game at a weekend tournament, especially when the former used the occasion of the task to grapple with a set of life-altering events, while the latter used it to demonstrate her ability to use twenty (or more!) vivid sensory images.

It is easy to understand writing as a product because products are visible. Meaning happens through the process of relating to a piece, and thought processes, like the process of writing, are invisible. Before I can make meaningful revisions to a piece, I need to think about a whole series of factors, from what I want to achieve, to what readers and reviewers might have said about my efforts, to the choices I could make to effect those changes. Based on these ideas, I began to have students build on what they learn during a reflection interlude to make explicit, written plans for revision.

In written revision plans, students must work to make the thinking behind their choices visible. In their plans, my students name what they will change about their writing, they describe the steps they will take or the strategies they will try to make those changes, and they work at articulating the reasoning behind these changes based on their goals and purposes for the piece, and whenever possible based on feedback they have received from or given to their peers. Doing this gives them a sense of agency and purpose for their writing. It teaches them to examine what they know, as well as to integrate new strategies and learning into their practice. When they are effective, these plans change how writers think about a piece of writing. Even ineffective plans can be helpful.

In my conference with Nick, the student writing about space trash, his plan served as a checkpoint and touchstone. I had taught a skill, for which he had reviewed another person's writing and reflected on his own. On reflection, he could see that he didn't understand that skill. When we looked at his plan, I saw that he and his reviewer had questioned two key points about the portion of the draft they had reviewed. The first had to do with his claim, which confused his reader. The second had to do with whether the evidence would work best as a quotation rather than as a paraphrase. He could see that he had not understood the skill I had hoped to teach; I could see the elements he needed to focus on to get there. Starting with the observation his reviewer had made about evidence, I was able to draw Nick's thinking out with a series of questions: How might stakeholders with different perspectives on space trash view that evidence? In what ways might their views relate to or contrast with the perspective you're expressing in your claim? What issues could you bring up that might connect your views to these alternate perspectives, and how could you connect those issues to your claim in a way that might reframe different readers' thinking?

Nick was able to revise his writing to clarify his claim and to develop reasoning that clearly connected the evidence to that claim. While this was not the goal I had hoped to teach, Nick was able to practice his way through a set of skills that would be essential to meeting that goal in the future. To be able to confer with Nick around questions like these in the context of a recognized and valued element—evidence—that another reader pointed out in his writing, gave him a sense of ownership over the possibility that the goal of the lesson was within reach. As we plan together, frequently, consistently, and over time, my students notice that they have learned to take ownership of their writing. They are thinking like writers.

Thinking in Cycles: From Feedback to Revision Plans

The writing process is often described as a series of steps. Writers brainstorm, draft, peer review, revise, edit, and publish. Peer review and revision are linked because it is incredibly difficult to imagine one's words from the point of view of a person who did not actually think those words. Having another person read something you wrote is the best way to find out whether you said what you thought. What I didn't realize before I started having students write revision plans, and what I still feel I am learning, is the importance of hearing an audience's reaction, receiving feedback from a reader, as only the entry point to the conversation writers have with themselves. Without some way to make it visible, revision remained nothing more than an assignment. I could tell my students what to fix, but to get them to think of making effective changes themselves was still as mysterious to me as it probably was to them.

Over the course of the 2015–16 school year, I spent some time with a teacher study group examining how to improve our students' feedback to one another. We noticed that in giving each other feedback, students revealed a lot about what they understood (or not) about elements of writing. Written peer reviews—artifacts of feedback—became valuable forms of assessment, and we worked to build a culture of collaboration and communication in our classrooms, teaching students to value the ways they read and responded to each other's work. This led me to the question of revision because I wasn't sure what choices students were actually making about their writing based on their peer reviews. My question became this: Based on comments from your reviewer or from things you noticed about the writing you reviewed, what will you add to, change, or cut out of your work? Working in an online platform, I began to require that they respond to these questions and to write their revision plans. I wasn't sure what would happen, but I hoped that seeing their thinking would help my students and me work together to better assess and evaluate what they understood about writing. Over time, however, patterns began to emerge. Students who talked about their choices in certain ways followed through and made significant, qualitative improvements to their drafts.

The turning point in noticing these patterns came as I was teaching students to develop their reasoning using a series of lessons from the National Writing Project's College, Career, and Community Writers Program. These lessons draw on the work of Joseph Harris and his book *Rewriting* (2006), in which he describes different reasoning moves writers might make to *forward* (his term) their arguments. My students had for some time demonstrated that they were proficient at the move Harris refers to as "illustrating," selecting evidence that supports their claim and providing commentary to clarify how and why the evidence provides this support. To move them beyond this, I had the class write source-based arguments on an assigned topic, school nutritional guidelines. I taught a revision lesson that focused on more sophisticated reasoning moves that Harris calls "countering" and "extending." Both of these moves involve selecting evidence that might be seen as providing more value to viewpoints other than one's own, and then using that evidence as a foundation to develop reasoning that reframes and redirects a reader's thinking.

Because the review and revision task in this case was limited and focused, by looking at the students' revision plans I could easily see both the moves effective planners made in their plans and how their plans then translated into significantly valuable changes to their drafts. Sarah, for example, was one of these early effective planners. After everyone in the class had tried making a plan, I shared her plan and her revisions with the class. Students noticed, first of all, that Sarah based her thinking on very specific comments from her reviewer, which she was able to do because her reviewer had avoided making broad statements. This observation helped to reaffirm for the class the value of good feedback. They also noticed when Sarah recognized strengths in her writing that her reviewer pointed out.

Sarah's reviewer had noticed her beginning to use extending and countering as reasoning strategies even in her rough draft, and in turn, Sarah had reflected on it in her revision plan. "This wasn't my original intention," she noted, "but it brought to my attention that I can tie my original idea of countering with extending. I didn't know I could do this, but apparently I did." Seeing that some parts of her draft were actually working better than she thought gave Sarah confidence to address some of the less successful parts as well. Writing about it in her plan helped

Note from Anne

It's worth noting that Derek's learning here is not something he undertakes alone. Just as his students need each other for plan revision, we teachers need colleagues to think with about how to revise our teaching. Both shared inquiry with a study group and interaction with others using the same materials supported Derek as he worked to strengthen students' capacities for revision.

her to reinforce her decision to move forward with
these revisions.

For example, Sarah's original draft had included evidence expressing the view that overly
strict guidelines would micromanage student eating
habits. In her reasoning in that original draft, she
had countered that this concern was "unreasonable"
because the guidelines would "only be taking place
during school" and not necessarily be "carried over
into home life." After the affirmation her reviewer
had given her and that she had taken the time to
recognize herself, she returned to her draft with the
intention of extending that idea. Thus, she revised
this passage of commentary to include the observations that even within strict guidelines, schools
offer students a variety of options and that parents
concerned about the guidelines would be free to
supplement students' school-time meals with other
kinds of food. In essence, she reframed the readers'
thinking by moving beyond her own assertion about
unreasonableness to point out that seeing guidelines as restrictions fails to consider
the benefits that drive their purpose. From there, she moved to a discussion of the
health impacts of childhood obesity. Her reasoning moved from a simple assertion of her opinion about an opposing viewpoint to reframing the concerns of the
evidence in a way that even people holding that viewpoint could share.

Most of my students initially saw revision as solely a process of fixing mistakes. Sarah saw it as more than that; she was a writer who invested herself in the
choices she made. Sharing Sarah's work with the class, seeing her process laid out
in front of them, showed students that revision could include improving assets, not
just addressing problems. I too began to see how planning led writers to literally
process what they had done well, naming what others had seen in their work and
using that understanding to say and show more. In the time and space that students
take to plan revisions, they reexamine their thoughts and generate clarifying ideas.
Pairing this time and space with specific instruction gives their thoughts direction.

Looking at what Sarah had done, my students also noticed that her plan
included critical reflections of her own about her work and that, further, Sarah
applied that thinking to her reviewer's comments. Sarah didn't just take every
reviewer comment at face value; she reflected on the meaning and value of a given
comment. For example, she wrote in her plan that "Libby's comment about how

she wasn't sure how my evidence tied to my explanation solidified my want [sic] to revise this section." It was also apparent, and somewhat surprising to her class-mates, that Sarah planned revisions by comparing her work to her partner's. For instance, they read Sarah's reflection that "Libby, in her paper, incorporated lots of anecdotal evidence I noticed. It made her paper seem more 'real' and human, less statistical." Most of the students in that class would have identified Sarah as one of the strongest writers in the class. It was eye-opening for the class to see how she looked to the work of a classmate who identified as a much weaker writer to improve her own work. Seeing this was also noteworthy for Sarah's partner.

Finally, one of the key points about effective revision plans like Sarah's was that writers actually played around with the revisions they planned to make. As Sarah considered how she wanted to improve her reasoning in one plan, she said, "I want to tie in the idea of micromanaging. Firstly starting with refuting the idea that an improved nutrition plan will micromanage every single aspect of what's served to children. This is simply untrue. The student still has the choice to choose their meal. . . ." The students and I saw this final move as a rehearsal, in which Sarah wrote in her plan a pre–rough draft of the revision she planned to make. In my classroom, writers who did this sort of rehearsal almost always followed through with changes when they revised.

From this point on, I began to teach students how to write revision plans by sharing a strong plan, like Sarah's, and having the class identify the thinking they noticed therein.

Positioning Writers to Look Forward in Meaningful Ways

Based on the work with Sarah and other writers like her, I worked with the class and with a pair of other educators to develop a rubric or scale that we could use together to evaluate the way my students were planning and to help them improve (Figure 8.1). My thinking was that if students who revised effectively planned in certain ways, teaching all students how to plan in those ways would help more of them revise effectively.

Along with looking at models of effective plans, using this scale has become part of my instructional practice. When we examine a strong plan at the beginning of the year, I make sure to identify where on the scale that plan falls. For example, I usually start the year by showing the students a "proficient" plan. The writer's moves are visible, but the possibilities that the writer discusses are not so various as to confuse emerging writers in the classroom who may lack confidence, or who may be uncertain about the purpose of writing itself, let alone the idea of revision. As they write their plans, I use this scale to assess, evaluate, and comment on the

Level	Descriptor of Proficiency	Moves to the Next Level
0–1	**Incomplete.** The plan names few choices. Choices that are named are unrelated to audience concerns, or to a sense of purpose for the writing, or to the purpose of the review task.	• Differentiate between strengths and weaknesses in the writing. • Name goals for addressing possible weaknesses and for building off of strengths.
2–3	**Partial.** The plan names choices or goals which may be linked to strengths and weaknesses of writing. The choices or goals may address audience concerns, a sense of purpose for the writing, and/or a sense of the purpose of the review task. Language is vague. The impact of the choices on the audience is implied.	• Explain strategies or steps to be taken to apply to changes within writing. • Connect additions, changes, or removals to specific comments from reviewers. • State an intended effect of revisions on the reader.
3–4	**Developing.** The plan names revision choices that are explicitly linked to audience concerns and to a sense of purpose. The plan names what revisions will be made and where in the draft they will occur. The plan names strategies that will be used, or names elements of writing that will be changed or added to achieve the revision goals. The plan explicitly considers intended effects of revisions on audience and makes links between these effects and the purpose of the writing. The language of the plan may be vague and descriptions of these elements may be general.	• When connecting additions, changes, or removals from specific comments from reviewers, offer reasoning for the value of the comment. • Use discipline-specific language to describe choices and intended effects on reader. • Clarify sense of purpose and connect the intended effects of revisions to purpose of the text. • Rehearse changes or additions.
5–6	**Proficient.** The plan describes revision choices that are explicitly linked to audience concerns through clear connections to specific reviewer comments. The plan describes where and how revisions in the draft will be made, commenting on the reasons for each choice in terms of specific audience concern and in terms of specific sense of purpose for each change. The plan generally uses discipline-specific vocabulary to name strategies and elements of writing. At times, the plan evaluates choices and reflects on reasons for selecting specific options among possibilities. The plan includes some possible rehearsals of changes or additions. At times, the plan articulates reasoning about revision choices in a way that demonstrates for the writer a sense of clarity and a sense of insight into goals and intended effects of choices on the audience. The clarifications and insights generated in the plan are linked at times to further options for revision, although these options may be implied, not named or explored.	• Evaluate options for achieving the intended effect of the choice on the audience when explaining how the choice impacts purpose. • Evaluate rehearsal of choices and consider alternate options. • Consider and compare multiple options to address specific concerns. • Reflect on strengths and weaknesses beyond those mentioned in review prompt. • Develop reasoning about choices based on prior experiences.

Figure 8.1. Proficiency levels for revision planning. (Developed by Derek Miller, Susan Wilson-Golab, and Melissa Meeks)

Figure 8.1. Continued

| 7–8 | **Advanced.** The plan describes a variety of possible choices and evaluates and explains the ranking and final selection of revisions to be made. The choices are linked to specific audience concerns based on clear connections to feedback, or to reflections on prior writing experiences. The plan incorporates commentary and reflection on the intended effects of revisions, linking them to purpose in a manner that intrinsically works to generate clarifications of thinking and insights that can lead to further options for revision, and sometimes describes and explains options for revision that extend from the process of planning itself. The plan includes rehearsals of changes, and at times includes multiple rehearsals of the same revision, evaluating the possibilities of achieving similar effects with different choices or changes. Choices, strategies, and intended effects are mostly described with concise, discipline-specific language. | |

thinking I see them doing, and to comment on ways they can improve their approach to their work. Sometimes the plans are graded, but only at the point in the year when I know that I can expect proficiency from my students and can effectively accommodate those who might still be struggling. Most important, I want my students to understand that planning, including planning for revision, is a valued part of writing.

We go back to our revision plans and use this scale throughout the year. Early on I share a variety of plans that, like Sarah's, have markers pointing toward successful revision—those in the 5–6 level. I model writing plans of my own, showing students feedback I have received from others (usually another teacher) and working through revision choices I am teaching them with my own writing. When I model, I share the questions I consider as I revise my work: *What does this feedback say about the reader's reaction? How*

Note from Anne

This account also highlights the principle that "assessment of writing involves complex, informed, human judgment." The Principles document elaborates on formative assessment, "provisional, ongoing, in-process judgments about what students know and what to teach next—assessments that may be complex descriptions and not reduced to a grade or score and that are intended to support students' writerly development" (p. xxiv). These assessments of revision plans are one such example. They provide information not on a piece of writing, but on a writer. Specifically, they reveal how well the writer has learned to engage in a process of planning for revision, one small unit in a complicated, interdependent system of skills and decisions that shape any one writer's process toward producing any one piece of writing.

is their reaction like or not like what I hoped it would be? What do I know that I could do to get this reader to think what I want? How can I use what I did well here in other parts of my draft? Based on what this reader said, what else do I know or understand about the purpose of my work?

Beyond looking at effective plans and using the scale to assess, evaluate, and comment on my students' plans, we spend time thinking and reflecting on our writing in a variety of other ways. As more students take up incorporating elements of effective planning into their own writing, we spend class periods looking at a range of plans, evaluating them with this scale and discussing particular qualities of each plan and how we might recognize those qualities as strengths. As the year moves forward and students grow in sophistication, we examine stronger plans. Showing them immediate examples from their classmates helps them to see that what they are doing is effective. They are able to relate directly to the tasks and compare the work we are examining to their own efforts. Over the course of this work, I make sure to remind students that although revision plans are written, it is the quality of thinking that matters.

Impacts on My Teaching

Writing is a process, as is learning how to write. Teaching people how to write is a process as well. In studying how to review, plan, and revise, my students and I both recognized and questioned some significant aspects of our practice even as we moved forward doing them. First of all, we had always written a lot in my classroom, but now my students were writing even more as they wrote their peer reviews and their revision plans. Very quickly I noticed that these informal artifacts gave me more immediately useful information about how much my students understood about the things I taught than I could learn from their drafts alone. This initially created some tension; we could all see that I was commenting more on the thinking they were doing than on their actual writing. To resolve this tension, I had to come back to my core principles, most specifically the principle that "writing is a process."

If I teach that process well, the writers in my classes will learn to create effective texts. When I teach my students to step aside from their writing, reflect on their feedback, and plan before they revise by modeling revision moves, by providing models of revision plans and examining them, and by teaching students to examine and compare their own work to these models, I am teaching writing as I know it from "the inside." Whether I am writing a poem for my son for his birthday, preparing notes for a professional development activity for my colleagues, or working on a chapter such as this for a professional publication, the time I spend committing text to page by literally typing or writing the words with a pencil is only a fraction of the larger span of inquiry, exploration, and creative decision making that goes into the finished product.

I have also learned from this teaching practice about the value of having a meta-understanding of writing processes. When I am purposeful in scaffolding the skills I teach and in designing review and revision tasks, I support my students' awareness and understanding of review and revision as writing processes. Each time they draft and review a piece, my students can see the repertoire of skills they have gained. When students' revision plans address possibilities, they show me they understand what I have taught, articulating how their final choice best suits their purpose far better than if I had simply taught a reasoning move and graded the students on whether they used it. This principle holds true for any element of writing, from evidence, to imagery, to structure in poetry, to elements of characterization in fiction. By composing a draft with multiple interludes in which they pause to review, reflect, and revise, my students experience multiple opportunities to practice and internalize the essential skills of being aware of their options, evaluating, and thinking critically about choices for how to achieve their purposes as writers. Externalizing their thoughts, they are able to internalize the process. They approach their tasks with purpose.

Signs of Growth

Growth happens over time. It was late April. My students had finished reading George Orwell's *1984*. They responded to the book with arguments, taking a stand that compared issues of technology and privacy and their impact on individuals in society today to the challenges faced by Winston and Julia living under the watchful eyes of Big Brother and the Thought Police. Concerns about Amazon Echo and Google Nest were all over the headlines. Facebook's privacy scandals were starting to break. Students had to support their arguments with evidence from the book and from current articles from periodicals and news outlets. Nick added comments to his plan like "I would also like to use authorizing, because one of my partners used it in their argument, and it made for great supporting evidence," showing that he was evaluating the success of his own work against choices his peers had made. In his revision, he even used this moment as a springboard to adding multiple perspectives to his reasoning, a step toward that extending move he had failed at some weeks earlier. For his part, Joe set goals to clarify evidence from a source in response to his reviewer's comment: "As Liam had stated I could try and expand more by including a statistic in regards to a real world piece of technology, like the license plate readers." These writers were thinking about their audience, comparing their work to others', and evaluating essential elements such as reasoning and evidence. Strong writers approach tasks with a wide variety of skills from which to choose, while weaker ones may have a more limited set. No matter what the writer's degree of skill, effective writing develops from the practice of making thoughtful choices. Practice happens over time. Like growth, it is a process.

Chapter Nine

Guiding Youth Voices: Teaching Students to Write for Many Audiences and Purposes

Paul Allison

Writing grows out of many purposes.

Everyone has the capacity to write; writing can be taught; and teachers can help students become better writers.

Note from Anne

As the Principles document states, "Writing grows out of many purposes," and other chapters in this book have illustrated the complexity of helping writers navigate processes of composing in relationship to their intended purposes and audiences. Here, Paul Allison describes one way he and colleagues have helped young writers tailor writing to their own purposes using "guides" based on analyses of other young writers' texts. He and his colleagues use these guides to support student writers in the spirit of the principle that "everyone has the capacity to write; writing can be taught; and teachers can help students become better writers." After a thirty-one-year career teaching English in New York City high schools, he now supports other teachers in their work as a tech consultant affiliated with the New York City Writing Project.

In Elaine Kouch's tenth-grade African American History class at Carver Engineering and Science High School in Philadelphia, students had just written comments to their peers on Youth Voices, a National Writing Project–sponsored website focused on digital writing and media making (youthvoices.live). They were now preparing posts about their own views on the American dream. Elaine had invited me, as a cofounder and manager of Youth Voices, into her classroom, and I sat beside one young man who had just finished drafting and revising a response to a piece by a student at Okemos High School in Michigan, where the racial breakdown is 64 percent White and 5 percent Black, the opposite of his own school, where 73 percent of his peers are Black and 5 percent are White. Kenneth had chosen a student post that he disagreed with, and he wanted to be sure that he wasn't offending anybody before posting his comment in reply. He wrote:

> Hey Owen,
>
> I have to say that I am deeply impressed by your article. I found it to be intelligently written, and I actually enjoyed reading it. It was very thought provoking. But, while impressed by the style of it, I have to admit that I do not agree with all of the content.
>
> First and foremost, I would like to address where you said, ". . . no matter if we're white, black, yellow, orange, tall, or short, we will always be given a chance to make the most out of our lives, we will always have opportunities—from pursuing any career you want to fulfilling your American Dream to living the way that you choose to live. . . ." While I do believe that this should be the case when discussing America and/or life in general, it simply isn't.
>
> There are many factors that hold black people back when it comes to succeeding. As a black person, I know that we endure tribulations that wouldn't even be considered as fathomable to most whites. To say that we all have equal opportunities in America while you know that racism is still prevalent (which I hope you do), is ignorant.
>
> I do like how you talked about how the American Dream is different for everybody. People tend to act like it should be the same for everyone, and I liked how you deviated from that ongoing (wrong) idea.
>
> I enjoyed your article as a whole. It was very mature and insightful. I would love to read more content from you.

How different his approach is from the trolling and abuse that is modeled so frequently on any number of online forums. Kenneth used a Youth Voices "guide" to help him write with purpose (of showing disagreement) while also establishing a positive relationship with his audience.

In this chapter, I describe how and why I and others in a group of National Writing Project (NWP) teachers have come together to create guides, in the context of building an openly networked site for youth writing and media making that has the marks of academic scholarship. Although conversation with an authentic audience of peers and others is central to this process, our guides are also important tools. Made directly from student writing, they assist young writers and producers in making significant connections with more experienced digital writers, which helps them to develop stronger arguments, more critical literary responses, and more engaging stories and poems. The point of this chapter is not to advertise for Youth Voices, but instead to show how it can at times, with care, be appropriate to develop a detailed guide for writers struggling to work in new genres and for new purposes and audiences.

This work exemplifies two key principles named in *Professional Knowledge for the Teaching of Writing*: "Writing grows out of many purposes" and "Everyone has the capacity to write; writing can be taught; and teachers can help students become better writers." First, we begin from awareness of the many purposes for writing, but we notice, as have so many students, that most often, the only purpose for writing in school is to show that you have learned to write. That is, too many school writing experiences are inauthentic, created for an audience of teachers or evaluators only. We looked for a forum in which to place student writers in direct communication with one another, and our result (but surely not the only place where student writers might communicate) was Youth Voices. On Youth Voices, as in other online spaces, students find many opportunities to write for a range of purposes outlined in the Principles, including

> developing social networks; reasoning with others to improve society; supporting personal and spiritual growth; reflecting on experience; communicating professionally and academically; building relationships with others, including friends, family, and like-minded individuals; and engaging in aesthetic experiences. (p. xii)

Second, we take the stance articulated in the Principles document that any writer can improve and that teaching makes a difference. When teachers from around the country—Chris Sloan, Susan Ettenheim, Lee Barber, Gail Desler, Natalie Bernasconi, Kiran Chaudhuri, and I—started building Youth Voices in 2003, our aim was to create a space where youth were really listening to one another and learning how to comment on each other's multimedia posts. From the beginning, we believed that authentic conversation could occur on a site developed by teachers and powered by youth.

Yet we found that our student writers needed some support in learning how to comment productively. Many of the models for online interaction that students might encounter in the world outside of

Note from Anne

Paul's point here reminds me how Sheridan Blau, author of *The Literature Workshop* (2003), characterizes most school writing assignments as "dry runs." That is, they tend to simulate things a student might do in the world with writing rather than taking the step of actually having a student do something with writing.

school, such as comments on news sites or on social media platforms, may indeed be authentic but are decidedly *not* models of respectful, productive interaction with an audience. In the spirit of supporting students, we decided to provide youth with guides to help them navigate Youth Voices and other digital environments like it. These scaffolds for writing help youth understand how to use new modalities for writing as they work with new publics, audiences, and purposes for composing.

When we create guides, we often begin with a particularly effective post that a student has published on Youth Voices. We copy all of that student's first, transitional, and concluding sentences, and we replace the content with suggestions for how novice or stuck writers might add their own content and details into the skeleton that we've built from the earlier, mentor post. These suggestions are put between angle brackets that youth are told to replace with their own writing. For example, anyone who has seen our "Agree/Disagree" guide would immediately recognize how carefully Kenneth, in the example quoted above, had stayed with the moves suggested there (see Figure 9.1).

By responding to the questions and suggestions in the Agree/Disagree Response guide (youthvoices.live/agreedisagree), Kenneth found a way to compose his complex and authentic reaction in a public online forum. Seeing his careful writing, I was reminded again of what Cathy Birkenstein and Gerald Graff have also found: "Far from turning students into mindless automatons, formulas like [these] can help [writers] generate thoughts that might not otherwise occur to them" (2008, p. 20). Formulas—when created mindfully and in connection with authentic texts—can be generative. In this case, a Youth Voices guide helped Kenneth to add his voice alongside another student's in a way that extends and invites dialogue.

Dear <First Name of Poster>:

I am <adjective showing emotion > <by, about, with> your <poem/post/image/letter . . .>, "<Exact Title>," because . . . <add 2 or 3 sentences>

One sentence you wrote that stands out for me is: "<Quote from message.>" I think this is <adjective> because . . . <add 1 or 2 sentences>

Another sentence that I <past tense verb> was: "<Copy a sentence or line from the post.>" This stood out for me because . . .

I <do/don't> <adverb> agree with you that . . . One reason I say this is . . . Another reason I <agree/disagree> with you is . . .

Figure 9.1. Excerpt from an Agree/Disagree comment guide.

The guides, while important, should be seen in the context of the complex social connections, the multiple modalities and technologies, and the important relationships between writers and readers. Guides like these are preceded by careful reading of models themselves, either writing of other students found at Youth Voices in similar interactions or models found in the broader "wild" of digital and/or print discourse. They are meant to make more explicit how a student might emulate a model, *not* to replace learning from analyzing model texts. Absent of this context, the guides would be easy to mistake for something else. They aren't mad libs (although what would be wrong with a little playfulness?), form letters (although maybe learning to write in some genres involves learning to use boilerplates), or cloze tests (although recognizing the kinds of words needed in particular contexts seems important). Instead, our work with guides is premised on a Connected Learning (clalliance.org/about-connected-learning) remix of James Moffett's theory of discourse, which argues that "ideally, a student would write because he was intent on saying something for real reasons of his own and because he wanted to get certain effects on a definite audience" (1968, p. 193). The guides also grew from our work to situate Sondra Perl's (1980) studies of composing processes in teaching novice writers and Peter Elbow's (1998) processes for generating, responding to, and revising writing into the new media world of online learning, digital writing, and social networks.

Note from Anne

When I first encountered this idea, I was skeptical. The notion of a detailed guide sounded a lot like the detailed "outlines" I had sometimes been handed as a student. These were decidedly not outlines for an argument I was formulating; they were just forms to fill out—and voila! An argument resulted. How would students learn these ways of writing, commenting, and so on if all they ever had to do was follow a guide, I wondered. But as Paul Allison explains, the key is that the guides are not handed to students as a priori formats, like recipes. Instead, they emerge after a firsthand study of some actual texts. It reminds me of geometry courses I took in high school, in that first we worked through the proof of a formula, but afterward we found it easier to simply memorize the formula. Or like cooking in your kitchen: If you were a beginner, you wouldn't expect to automatically internalize a recipe for, say, cake frosting. The first few times you made it, you'd likely refer to the recipe. Later on, with experience and having tried many kinds of frosting, you'd have internalized enough to just make your own without a reference, or even to "wing it" with varied ingredients.

By themselves, these guides might seem to a student like little more than prompts to perform for a teacher, but when used in the context of authentic exchange—writing for the real audience on Youth Voices and drawing on the writing of other students who have posted there—the guides become "just-in-time" sources of help for finding appropriate languages for composing within the complex social relationships that grow between peers on Youth Voices.

For example, recently, in a classroom for multilingual language learners, I was called over by one of our students, Jai, an unaccompanied youth from India. He was composing an essay that he wanted to publish about the positive and

Note from Anne

There's a kind of generosity in helping a student get started. Jai clearly has much to say, and Paul has handed him a tool for getting some of it onto paper. As I reflect on this, I am mindful of how many times I have let students struggle with getting started. I have done this in the name of independence—I want them to write their own ideas, not ideas I supply. I also have let them struggle out of my conviction that learning to stick with struggle is an important part of learning to write. After all, I think much of the difference between a successful writer and an unsuccessful writer is simply that the successful writer was able to endure and move through the struggle well enough to get some writing done, period, while the other writer stopped. Yet in letting student writers struggle, I have also sometimes let them stop altogether. Paul's practice of providing very specific guides makes me take a closer look at the blurry line between helping too much and not helping enough.

negative impacts of technology, and he was having difficulty. "Can you just start this paragraph for me?" he asked. "Then I think I can finish it."

It seemed to me that Jai had lost track of why he was writing this piece and who his audience was. I reminded him that he was writing about a topic that he had chosen. We looked back at his early freewriting on his questions. We also looked at the comments he had previously written to others who had posted about the effects of technology on our lives. Next, we reviewed his annotations on articles he had read. Then, within that context of his own ideas and the writing he and others had already produced in the conversation he wished to extend, I pointed him to our guide for Personal Inquiry that gave him specific language for pulling together his question, his research, and his desire to enter conversations with his peers. All of these helped Jai to understand what he needed to produce, and the guide gave him a scaffold for the how.

Principled Teaching with Guides

In the more than fifteen years that we've been making these documents, we've created more than seventy-five guides for the following: Assessment and Reflection, Commenting, Structured Essays, Literature Response, Multimedia Response, Non-Fiction Text Response, Poems and Stories. They are all available from the navigation bar at the top of Youth Voices.

Ultimately, we provide this scaffolding out of a conviction that "everyone has the capacity to write; writing can be taught; and teachers can help students become better writers." Guides scaffold students in learning how to do this. Just as coaches help young athletes to grow stronger through both public performance and careful practice, we can help students become better writers by providing them with the coaching they need to be successful in these multimodal public spaces.

High school writers often have spent years writing repeatedly in school genres such as the timed short essay found on tests to the exclusion of experiences writing in other genres or in purposes other than proving that they possess skills. When faced with more authentic writing situations, such as the invitation to write for internet radio, students often struggle to discern what structures make sense for these new purposes and the genres that grow out of them. If it's true that "writing grows out of many purposes," and if the goal is for youth to emerge from high school with skills that will serve them as they move on to contexts beyond school after graduation, they will need experience in observing and analyzing how other writers do things and borrowing from other authors as they seek to structure their own texts. Thoughtfully constructed guides that are built from authentic student writing can provide scaffolding for youth to compose within the conventions of a variety of genres and their discourse communities.

Note from Anne

Your students are welcome to start publishing and commenting on Youth Voices, and you can start sharing your own guides alongside the student work upon which guides are based. Visit youthvoices.live/ for more information.

Part II: Concluding Thoughts

There is value to articulating principles as a source for reflection, consideration, and analysis. However, any classroom teacher has to ask, What does this look like in the classroom with actual students? In these chapters, you've heard from teachers in their own voices, writing about their classroom practices in relationship to principles from the Principles document. Some of these are long-standing practices that teachers began to see in a new way; others are new practices these teachers have developed.

All of the teacher–authors engaged in a similar process to produce these chapters. They were asked to read and reflect on the Principles document and think of a snapshot into their classroom practice that would show how one or more of those principles were alive in the classroom. When I work with groups of teachers in a professional development session or a graduate course, we approach things in a way very similar to what these teacher–authors have done. Recall that in the introduction to Part II, I suggested reflecting on each chapter, perhaps in writing, with these questions in mind:

- How does this person's teaching or setting remind you of your own? How is it different? What do you make of the similarities and differences?

- What surprises you in this teacher's account? Why is it surprising, and what can you learn from the surprise?

- Where do you see the principle that the author identifies coming through in their description of practice?

Now would be a good time to read back over your notes. One of my favorite things about writing as a way of thinking is how it adds such layers to thought: we think about something, we write about that thinking, we think about that writing, we gain further insight into that "something" as well as into our writing and even ourselves.

As you review your readings of the chapters, try this sequence of prompts for reflection:

- When you read over all of your reactions to the chapters, what words or phrases do you notice you are repeating? What do you make of that repetition? Jot a list, or if you prefer, let it all out in a quick-write.

- When you read over all of your reactions to the chapters, what questions can you formulate? These may be questions you wish you could ask the authors, but they may also be questions you find you're asking *yourself* after reading. Jot a list, or if you prefer, let it all out in a quick-write.

- Is there a particular principle from the Principles document that the teacher-authors took up that really resonates with you? Why? What is it activating for you? Jot some notes, or try a quick-write.

- Go back to the Principles document. Reread the description of that resonating principle, along with the text beneath it about what it means for the classroom. What are you noticing in the *Professional Knowledge for the Teaching of Writing* text that you hadn't noticed before? Or, what words are standing out in a new way? Or, what questions do you have? Jot some notes or try a quick-write.

- You might even take up the prompt that invited these chapters: Take one or two of these principles. Write a snapshot of what it looks like in your classroom. (Or, write a snapshot of what it could look like in your classroom. What would be the ideal? How might you take a step or two toward that ideal?) Then, think about where that practice came from, or why you do it the way you do. How did your embrace of that principle grow to this point? Where might it grow even more?

None of this reflective work on its own magically changes the way we teach. But what it can do is focus our attention in the direction of growth. It can tickle that productive dissatisfaction, that inkling that we feel when new growth in our practice is coming. I've made the case that viewing our teaching helps us grow our practice right alongside the growing writers we teach. To extend that line of thought, let's take a look in Part III at how professional knowledge grows. Where might your learning lead you next?

III Growing On
from Here

Growing Your Own Professional Knowledge as a Teacher of Writing

H ow simple it would be if you could just learn everything you need-ed to know about teaching writing at the university, when you were preparing to be a teacher. Then you'd arrive in the classroom ready to go, knowing what you need to know, and that would be that. Sometimes policymakers seem to believe this is how it works. But teachers know better. One of the main activities of teaching is . . . learning. Our professional knowledge grows with time, but time alone isn't magic.

How did Jenell Penn figure out that Mondays were special? How did Derek Miller come to his practice of having students write revision plans rather than simply commanding, "Revise!," and how did he learn to connect those plans to reflective interludes? What did Paula Uriarte try before she had the murder mystery idea, and how did she know she had hit on something useful when she imagined it for the first time?

These teachers weren't just lucky. Nor, let's note, did they just receive commercial packages from administrators that neatly did the trick. No, they learned through years of professional development experiences, both the ones provided by their schools and the ones they sought out on their own. They learned from colleagues and from the writing and research produced by both teaching colleagues and their university-based counterparts. And they learned from their own experiences as writers and as participants in writing communities. In this chapter, we'll look more closely at ways to develop your own professional knowledge as a teacher of writing so that your teaching can live into your principles as fully as possible.

How Professional Knowledge Grows

Synthesizing decades of research on the professional development of teachers, Desimone (2011) offers a list of key characteristics of professional development experiences that significantly impact teachers' learning and practice. In the pages that follow, I suggest ways these characteristics fit with our own professional knowledge growth as writing teachers.

Content Focus

Experiences should be tied to some specific content and how students learn in that content area. One implication of this is simply that if we want to get better at teaching writing, we need to dedicate some of our professional learning time and energy to learning about the teaching of writing in particular. Perhaps this seems obvious, but the truth is that many teachers enter the profession without a dedicated course on the teaching of writing (Hochstetler, 2007; Smagorinsky, 1995), and many may not encounter further support after that. For knowledge in the teaching of writing to grow, you'll have to focus on writing.

I've sometimes seen writing teachers get so involved in what they were teaching students to write *about* (usually works of literature, but sometimes some other shared material, whether it's environmental justice, or community history, or anything you care to build a unit around) that they seem to forget that writing itself is a content. That is, there is knowledge to be had about writers, writing processes, and how to engage with those that a teacher of writing can intentionally develop. One way might be to conduct teacher research in your own classroom, examining some aspect of your students' activities as writers. Another might be to read current professional literature and research, or follow blogs dedicated to the teaching of writing (see the annotated bibliography that follows this chapter for ideas). Finally, the best way to engage the content of writing is . . . by writing. That's right; YOUR writing matters. Is there a creative writing course you might enjoy, locally or online? A community writing group, perhaps at your local library? Or maybe you can open each of your days with "morning pages" (Cameron, 2016), in which you simply write what comes to mind as a kind of meditation for you the writer and you the person. Try writing what you are asking students to write: even if you don't complete each assignment, even beginning pieces with the class will help you connect to the intellectual work that is involved. I'll say a lot more about writing as a teacher later in this chapter.

Active Learning

Maybe you, like me, have attended "professional development" sessions in which a speaker lectured or a video was shown, after which all the teachers left the room and went home. Research shows that for professional learning experiences to make a difference, they must involve some chance to work with the material. Maybe you bring some student work and look at it together in light of what a speaker has just said. Maybe you dig into some curricular materials to do some planning. Maybe you try out a strategy and receive some feedback on what you did. But simply passively listening—or even passively reading a book like this one—isn't enough to make a difference in writing instruction.

So what would make a difference? Try inviting an instructional coach, colleague, or even enlightened administrator into your classroom for some insight. Declare Fridays to be "new idea days," and choose something each week from a slice of professional reading (maybe this book!) to experiment with in your classes. When you find yourself in a required professional development session, take notes and then go out with a colleague afterward to plan ways of trying out what was suggested. Listening to someone talk about teaching, while sometimes provocative, almost never provokes real change in what you do day to day unless you make deliberate efforts to *do* what you're learning about right away.

Coherence

Coherence in professional development means that what you learn needs to make sense in context of the other things you know, experience, and believe. I see coherence as one of the toughest challenges to helping teachers improve their writing instruction, because so many times policy or local procedure stand counter to what we know from research is most effective for our students.

For example, we know that genres emerge from disciplinary communities, and so what counts as "good writing" will vary from science, to history, to literature, and so on—right down to conventions like how sources should be cited or what verb tense should be used. Yet in one high school I taught in, teachers were handed a set of common writing rubrics to use across all subject areas; the rubrics were almost verbatim from the state exam rubrics for writing an argumentative essay. How incongruent these were with my values of authenticity, with my knowledge of disciplinary writing communities, and with my hopes to see students writing in a range of genres for a range of audiences!

Our professional learning experiences need to fit, not contradict. When policies at the national, state, or local level layer on multiple frameworks and tools for us to use, sometimes our inclination is to find a way to integrate them all. But truly, some things cannot be integrated. I can't reconcile having all students in a class write in support of the same teacher-provided thesis sentence, for example, as one of my next-door teachers used to do, if I also value writing as helping students to discover and promote their own ideas. If I believe that writing experiences should be as authentic as possible, it gets more and more difficult to give my students "test prep" tasks like dry runs for timed essays in response to short stories. Nowhere in adult life—or in a kid's life out of school—does someone hand you a random story and say "Thirty minutes! Multiparagraph response! GO!"

When choosing among professional development options, go for choices that promise to strengthen your ability to teach in a way that fulfills your goals and values, not weaken them. Sometimes you can't choose, such as when your school requires all teachers to attend something. But you *can* filter new ideas against principles stated in the Principles document, calling into question recommendations or mandates that don't fit with the consensus norms of our field. You can use these to integrate material where possible and reject other material.

Duration

Desimone (2011) found that professional development should spread over a semester or more and should involve at least twenty hours of contact time. That is, one state-mandated day is not going to change much.

If you do have a one-day learning experience, such as attending a thought-provoking session of some kind or a weekend conference such as the NCTE Annual Convention or that of one of its many state affiliates, you'll get more out of it if you can continue the journey in some way. Perhaps a group of friends can agree to meet monthly over coffee to share some follow-up reading and conversation. Perhaps you can invite a thinking partner to conduct a shared inquiry sparked by the session. Perhaps you'll journal for a few minutes each day during planning period about how something you learned is playing out day to day. Perhaps you'll go back and share with your department colleagues, who then decide to implement something new together. The key is to engage with what you are learning over time.

Collective Participation

Finally, research shows that effective professional development follows from collective participation. This means it works better when we gather with other teachers with whom we have something in common: members of a school, department, or other preexisting group, or perhaps people we are meeting for the first time but with whom we have a common interest, such as all teaching high school writers or all working in schools with many English learners. This one just makes sense: we learn better in community, when we have someone to provoke our thinking or to ask questions with. Later in this chapter, we'll explore ways to find your collective even when your school doesn't provide one for you.

Your Own Writing Matters

When it comes to growing professional knowledge for teaching writing, your own writing life really matters too. Have you ever seen a swimming coach who didn't know how to swim? It's a silly idea, but so many writing teachers never write themselves. Sometimes it's that we don't seem to find the time (and in the next few pages, I'll share some ideas about how to make the time you need for writing). Sometimes it's that we have learned to dislike writing, or to doubt our own abilities as writers—usually back when we were students ourselves.

Facing these issues and claiming our own right to write is central to becoming the best teachers of writing we can be. Since this truth is both so simple and so very difficult to practice, I want to dwell for a while on how and why our own writing lives *have* to connect to the work that we do with students.

Why

Research has shown that our writing identities as teachers influence our effectiveness as teachers of writing. This happens for many reasons. First of all, finding ourselves in writing situations, having trouble with those, and having to figure out what to do helps us better understand what challenges students might face when they are writing. This increases our empathy for students. It also helps us to foresee what they might need and to then prepare appropriate supports, such as mini-lessons or resources for them to use.

Second, when we are writers and can share our writing experiences with students, it places us alongside the students. Of course we're still in authority over them, and of course we still have responsibilities as the adult in a relationship, but in an important way, being writers with the kids makes us their peer. We're a fellow writer, engaged in a parallel struggle. Even if we are more experienced and have more resources to draw on, our relationship to student writers becomes closer through writing.

What

What might you write? The truth is, it doesn't matter what you write so much as it matters *that* you write. Many teachers find it useful to write alongside their students, engaging in the very tasks they have placed in front of students. Even if you don't take a draft all the way through the process to publication, it can be extremely useful to try to do the assignments you make for your students. One group of teachers I worked with decided to do this together over the course of a school year as a group. As a school grade-level team, they wrote through each of the major assignments that they shared as an English department. This led to many new ideas about how to better support students along the process of doing those tasks themselves, and in some cases, that in turn led the teachers to revise the tasks for their students.

Most teachers also find it useful to write about their teaching. I'll say more about this later in this chapter, but try this: When students are writing in your classroom, look around. What do you see? What writer do you notice? Or what writer have you not noticed lately whom you could focus on for a while? Classroom writing time for the kids is also writing time for *you* to make your own notes and engage in some reflection. You can steal these writing minutes from the teaching day and get benefits that flow directly back into your teaching.

The writing that teachers do is as varied as the teachers who do it. Teachers I know write poems, stories, memoir, or reflections on their own families and children. They write conference presentations and grant proposals for their classrooms. They write articles for publications such as *English Journal* describing their teaching and asking questions about it that help colleagues. They write letters to family members, letters to the editor, letters to elected representatives. All of this writing feeds back into how we work with students.

When

Teachers are under tremendous time pressure. In fact, so are almost all Americans, as beautifully discussed by Brigid Schulte in *Overwhelmed: Work, Love, and Play When No One Has the Time* (2014). Drawing on time use research, Schulte explains how almost all of our time, whatever activity we are engaging in, is invaded by awareness and often worry about other activities that also need attention. The result is that our work, play, and even time with those we love is of degraded quality, our minds divided between the present moment and our sense of the scarcity of time.

There is only one way out of this trap. Time can be scarce, it's true, but we can decide to simply be in one place at a time, doing one thing at a time. Writing does not have to take long. And we don't need to spend time getting ready to do it, either. Think of the short bursts of writing time your students get in class, for a quick-write or to work on something on their own. Sometimes it's just seven minutes, right? "Take out your notebooks," you might say, and then you expect them to jump in. Well, we can do the same. We can open our own notebooks, right then when the kids do, and make a few notes or some stream-of-consciousness mind dumping. We can have a notebook in our bag so that when waiting at an appointment, or outside one of our own children's activities, or in the library before the faculty meeting begins (or even . . . shh! . . . during the meeting, depending on what's going on), we can write. We can write for ten minutes in the empty classroom just after the students leave, processing this day for a moment before jumping into preparation for the next. We can write "morning pages" (Cameron, 2016) over coffee, or list some gratitudes before heading up to bed.

With Whom

Almost everything goes better with a partner. Writing partners can be people you coauthor writing with, but they can also be accountability partners, like the friend you arranged to go to the gym with. You don't skip that workout, because you don't want to stand up your friend. I know teacher-writer partners who meet before or after school to check in about whether and what they write that day. I know partners who meet in an empty classroom once a month, and another group who meet at a local coffee shop very early on Saturday mornings, just to write quietly together. The presence of the others keeps them mostly on-task; afterward, they might go for a drink or order a bite to eat. If you have a National Writing Project site in your area, it already has a rich community of teachers writing together for weeks each summer, throughout the year in writing groups, at "writing marathons" in museums or around town, and more. All you have to do is contact them and ask how you can be involved.

Who are your people? Is there a like-minded teacher on your team or in your building? A friend from college or from a graduate course you took? Maybe your significant other is interested in writing too, or one of your own children. All it takes is an invitation, however awkward it may feel the first time, to ask someone to meet and spend time writing.

> **For further reading:**
>
> These resources speak directly to how teacher-writers can get together and work together, as well as give advice about what and how to write.
>
> Damico, N., & Whitney, A. E. (2017). Turning off autopilot: Mindful writing for teachers. *Voices from the Middle, 25*(2), 37–40.
>
> Dawson, C. M. (2016). *The teacher-writer: Creating writing groups for personal and professional growth.* Teachers College Press.
>
> Hicks, T., Whitney, A. E., Fredricksen, J., & Zuidema, L. (2016). *Coaching teacher-writers: Practical steps to nurture professional writing.* Teachers College Press.
>
> Locke, T. (2015). *Developing writing teachers: Practical ways for teacher-writers to transform their classroom practice.* Routledge.
>
> Whitney, A. E. (2009). Opening up the classroom door: Writing for publication. *Voices from the Middle, 16*(4), 17–24.
>
> Whitney, A. E. (2012). Lawnmowers, parties, and writing groups: What teacher-authors have to teach us about writing for publication. *English Journal, 101*(5), 51–56.

"Writing" Your Own Professional Growth Story

Almost every teacher wants to grow in professional expertise, and yet too many times, the learning opportunities provided to teachers are terribly thin, possessing none of the qualities outlined above. The good news is that we don't have to work solely with what is required, or what is offered by our employers, if that's not what we need. We can write our own stories of professional learning. This might involve building a learning community in your own school or with NCTE colleagues, selecting professional learning opportunities that make sense given your own goals and these principles, and making use of writing activities to grow as a teacher of writing. What can you do now to better connect your own practice to principles? To engage in meaningful professional activities that grow you as a teacher of writing as well as growing your students as writers?

By now I hope I've made the case that writing can be an important part of your professional life. Take up a notebook (or open a document) now and spend some time writing to plan the next steps in your professional journey. You won't want to do all of this in one sitting. Maybe you'll set aside a few minutes each morning, or each night before bed. Maybe a group of friends will take a few Saturday mornings to gather for coffee and reflective writing. However you approach it, the goal here is to let the act of writing open up your mind and heart about what might make teaching better for you and make you a better teacher.

Notice the difference between those? So often our focus is, rightly, on how what we do will impact the students in our classroom. Of course that is important. But *you* are also important. It's important how you feel when teaching, who you get to be in your profession. It's important how your energy is replenished, how your heart is nourished, given the many ways teaching can be draining. It's important that you be aware and in control of at least some aspects of your work, even when so much of what we do comes fast and uncontrollable. And it's important that you have the knowledge and skills you need to feel that you're able to do the good work that's in front of you, feeling the daily challenge of teaching but also knowing that you're standing on solid ground. These bursts of writing can help you look at your teaching through these eyes, eyes that look not only at students but also at you and at the whole endeavor of being a teacher. Ultimately, when we can connect our personal experiences and practice to our professional knowledge and practice, we are best equipped to teach with principle and with resilience, for the benefit of our student writers.

Prompts for professional reflective writing:

About your teaching life in general

- **Time Inventory:** Where does your time go? Note your activities—and your feelings as you engage those activities—over a day or a week. What does this inventory help you to notice?

- **Wonderings:** What are you curious about? As things happen in your teaching day or week, what questions can you ask about them?

- **Wishes:** What do you wish would happen? Or if you had a magic wand, how might you change a classroom situation? This can sometimes open up solutions by helping you view situations with less self-judgment and guilt.

- **Resources:** Many times we feel that we are alone in teaching or that we have to work through things on our own. Yet usually there are people and resources that we are not drawing upon. Who are my people, and what are my resources? Make a list of people you might reach out to or other resources you might consult.

About teaching writing in particular

- **Day in the life/week in a life:** Narrate the life of your writing class. What is this a story about?

- **Shadowing:** Choose a focal student writer in your class and spend a week noting what that writer says and does. What do you learn about this writer or about your class?

- **Fly on the wall:** Invite a guest teacher, colleague, or instructional coach to lead your class. You can observe without talking. Then write about what you noticed when you were able to be in the room in a quieter role.

- **Students' wishes:** Have the kids make writing wish lists, brainstorming ideas for things they'd like to try to write in the future. Read through these lists and compare them to a list of your own: what students have written or what you have planned for them this year. What differences do you see? Could you bring them closer?

- **Focal principle:** Each day choose a principle to focus on. Write it on a sticky note and keep it somewhere you'll see all day. At the end of the day, do some writing: What did you notice related to this principle this day? How was it alive in your classroom? Or in conflict? Or absent?

Once you've engaged in this kind of writing for a while, you can read back over what you have. What can you discern as needs or wishes for your own professional growth? How might you pursue growth in those directions?

Annotated Bibliography
David Premont

Books

Anderson, Carl
A Teacher's Guide to Writing Conferences
Heinemann, 2018

There is a lot to admire about the way Carl Anderson approaches writing conferences and the way he organizes his book. One of the most important takeaways is the idea that writing conferences are not inherent to teachers—there are "moves" teachers must make in order to create a successful conference. Anderson describes some of the moves teachers can make given the various situations and scenarios that student writers find themselves in. For example, he suggests that teachers focus on one specific writing move a student can make in various scenarios, but he explicitly suggests doing this when a student thinks the writing is "done." Beyond the craft that Anderson teaches, the book is just delightful, written with a blend of traditional prose and engaging graphics, along with cartoon illustrations of possible writing conference approaches and scenarios. The author also includes multiple videos of himself in the act of a writing conference, sharing his analysis of the conference as well.

Burke, Jim
The Six Academic Writing Assignments: Designing the User's Journey
Heinemann, 2019

Jim Burke provides insightful commentary and thoughts on his research about the writing that secondary ELA students are traditionally tasked with. He believes that the overwhelming majority of secondary writing activities fall within six types: (1) writing to learn, (2) short answer, (3) writing on demand, (4) the process paper, (5) the research paper, and (6) alternative forms. Burke walks the reader through each of these activities and provides examples of the way he approaches them in his classroom—including the way he scaffolds feedback—while providing scoring guides and sample handouts along the way. His focus on developing writers by helping them learn the moves that successful writers make through engaging writing activities is admirable. Particularly compelling is the yearlong project Burke invites his students to undertake, researching a self-chosen topic for the majority of the school year. This activity not only challenges students but also enables them to engage meaningfully in one topic for an extended period. The book includes activities and ideas that are adaptable to many classrooms.

Culham, Ruth
Teach Writing Well: How to Assess Writing, Invigorate Instruction, and Rethink Revision
Stenhouse, 2018

Ruth Culham invites teachers to envision new ways of responding to student work and helping them understand the power of revision. I especially appreciated her emphasis on "an inch wide and a mile deep" in her writing approach. This book is easily adapted to all secondary levels and abilities. Culham shares strong definitions and examples of the writing traits, how to implement strong teaching of the writing traits in various modes and genres, and the power of giving students autonomy to make writerly decisions. Replete with resources designed to help practicing teachers, the book includes examples of scoring guides that are easily adapted to meet the needs of various classrooms, handouts of friendly writerly reminders, and a table of picture books as mentor texts organized by writing trait.

Dawson, Christine M.
The Teacher-Writer: Creating Writing Groups for Personal and Professional Growth
Teachers College Press, 2016

The ideas, contents, and practices described in Christine M. Dawson's book have strong implications beyond the concerns of teacher educators and practicing English language arts teachers—that is, her underlying emphasis is on the personal and professional growth associated with consistent writing. Dawson and her writing group open conversations about and explore the possibilities of the writing educators can undertake that is designed primarily for the self—for personal or professional purposes. Because each member of the writing group had work and familial responsibilities, there were no set expectations for the group beyond their regularly scheduled two-hour, biweekly online meeting. Thus, members could arrive with a piece of writing at any stage of the writing process, or even without writing if necessary. The power of the writing group was found not only in personal writerly decisions—audience, genre, and ideas—but also in the talk demonstrated at each meeting. Members of the group refined through talk writing designed to repair broken friendships, writing that served as a toast at a wedding, and a found poem about a life well lived, for example. Dawson's book reminds us that writing can and ought to be for the self, for reasons beyond the academic, and acknowledges the power that accompanies such writing.

Dean, Deborah
Strategic Writing: The Writing Process and Beyond in the Secondary English Classroom (2nd ed.)
National Council of Teachers of English, 2017

As a former student of Deborah Dean's, I can confirm that this book embodies her approach to and beliefs about writing. Dean intentionally introduces a number of strategies for student writers to consider at various stages of the writing process. She outlines strategies such as talking, reading, and, yes, even writing as a way to "come

to know." But the strategies do not stop there: Dean actively walks the reader through drafting strategies, demonstrating how considering audience and purpose can strengthen the focus of the writing, as well as revision strategies, both holistic and sentence-level. As if that's not enough, Dean includes a treasure trove of lesson plans in the appendixes, where readers can examine how she envisions these ideas coming together during classroom instruction.

Fecho, Bob
Writing in the Dialogical Classroom: Students and Teachers Responding to the Texts of Their Lives
National Council of Teachers of English, 2011

"I'm urging those of us who teach to get in over our heads with explorations into who we are becoming, and that reading, writing, speaking, and listening be the means for doing so" (p. 5). Defining writing in the dialogical classroom is hard to deconstruct in one or two sentences, but to help readers understand his vision, Bob Fecho carefully leads us into the classrooms of six practicing teachers and the ways they implement writing in dialogical spaces. What resonates with me about these approaches are the opportunities students have to write about their families, their culture, their interests, and their passions in ways that naturally require critical thinking, autonomy, and engagement with texts. Not only does such writing ignite student passion, but it also affords the context and clarity that teachers need to more meaningfully connect with students. I was overwhelmed with the powerful implications such instruction leads to.

Gallagher, Kelly, and Penny Kittle
180 days: Two Teachers and the Quest to Engage and Empower Adolescents
Heinemann, 2018

Two of the most well-known ELA practitioners have teamed up to coauthor a book that outlines each unit and big idea they implemented during the 2016–17 school year. Kelly Gallagher and

Penny Kittle offer readers a glimpse into their classrooms and the emphasis they both place on regular reading, writing, and student conferencing. Particularly impressive is the collaboration Gallagher and Kittle worked out between their respective classrooms, where students could learn from one another and gain perspectives foreign to their own. There is much to admire about the way Gallagher and Kittle share their writing experiences with students, demonstrating that they are learners too. And, while these master teachers are composing along with their students, they make sure to invite them to write about topics that are prevalent in society or of general interest to students. This coauthored classroom has inspired other teachers to consider a model similar to Gallagher and Kittle's, enriching their students' literacy experiences as well.

Lindblom, Ken, and Leila Christenbury
Continuing the Journey 2: Becoming a Better Teacher of Authentic Writing
National Council of Teachers of English, 2018

Ken Lindblom and Leila Christenbury have designed a wonderful companion book for authentic writing instruction in secondary schools. I feel this book is best shared with preservice teachers as it provides a nice overview of writing from a variety of perspectives. A common element specific to their book series is the From the Teachers' Lounge vignettes by a variety of teachers and teacher educators who share anecdotal writing experiences and the way they approach writing in their individual classes. Additionally, Lindblom and Christenbury address strategies that are important for preservice teachers to consider as they work to provide a writing curriculum that lends authenticity to student writing in a way that acknowledges important considerations such as audience. They also address strategies and approaches for handling the daunting challenge of providing feedback to student writers. The format of the book allows readers to learn about a variety of approaches from various writing teachers.

Rief, Linda
The Quickwrite Handbook: 100 Mentor Texts to Jumpstart Your Students' Thinking and Writing
Heinemann, 2018

Linda Rief has compiled a beautiful collection of mentor texts composed by former students, colleagues, and professional writers (including herself) that she calls quickwrites. She encourages her students to write quickly—two to three minutes only—about the mentor text under consideration. The benefits of the quickwrites are plentiful, allowing students to play with the writing, learn the craft from strong writing, and write about topics and ideas that are important to them and the world around them. Alongside most quickwrites, Rief shares a few approaches teachers can take with that particular piece to engage students in thinking and writing.

Rubenstein, Susanne
Speak for Yourself: Writing with Voice
National Council of Teachers of English, 2018

Over the years, I have heard and experienced the challenging nature of strong teaching practices that enhance a writer's voice. Susanne Rubenstein's book provides a much needed resource for secondary teachers because it challenges the status quo by encouraging teachers to make voice a primary consideration in writing instruction. Rubenstein likens voice to the choices writers make, claiming that it's an inescapable aspect of decision making. There's no simple way to teach voice within writing, she argues—it's the culmination of reading multiple works by well-established writers and discovering how they bring out their voice in their writing. She encourages writers to examine the unique voice of professional writers to discover what they have to offer in terms of writing instruction. Rubenstein also admits that voice is hard to assess, and rightfully so. Because voice is so hard to capture, Rubenstein believes that it ought to be an integral aspect of writing instruction throughout the year, with the teacher modeling and validating its importance regularly. It should permeate students' writing to the point that they "can't imagine a piece of writing—and that includes the writing they do—existing without" (p. 120).

Smagorinksky, Peter
Teaching English by Design: How to Create and Carry Out Instructional Units (2nd ed.)
Heinemann, 2018

Peter Smagorinsky's book is replete with practical instructional material for secondary ELA teachers and composed with a wit that we've become accustomed to in his works. Though this book is not explicitly focused on writing instruction, it includes multiple chapters about writing instruction and how that fits in the larger context of a unit. Smagorinsky divides this section into multiple parts: goals for conventional and unconventional assessments and responding to student writing. I found particularly insightful the section on unconventional writing assessment, in part because the "schoolishness" of the activities is absent and authenticity is increased. It's also worth noting that each chapter has a brief section on how preservice teachers might include this information in a performance assessment (e.g., edTPA), and there is a more detailed chapter about performance assessment preparation toward the final remarks. Smagorinsky does not mince words when he explains how he feels about performance assessment tests, but he also provides sound counsel to preservice teachers by sharing strategic approaches to such a task.

Whitney, Anne Elrod, Colleen M. McCracken, and Deana Washell
Teaching Writers to Reflect: Strategies for a More Thoughtful Writing Workshop
Heinemann, 2019

The underlying premise of this book has strong implications for every ELA classroom from the youngest elementary students to preservice ELA teachers, even though it's designed primarily for elementary school audiences. Anne Whitney and colleagues effectively demonstrate the connection between reflection and writing growth as they take us into an elementary school classroom and engage with teachers and students. The strategies and approaches they use to teach students to reflect enable students to *identify* as writers. Whitney and colleagues explain that their invitation for students to reflect must be taught. So they dedicate time to "zoom out" on writing activities, asking students questions that allow them to consider who they are becoming as writers—questions such as explaining what they have tried, how they thought about the writing, and why they made certain decisions. Together, these reflections aid students in their writing goals and provide memories that students can draw from in future writing activities.

Online Resources

Literacy & NCTE
http://www2.ncte.org/blog/

Another resource worth checking out is the writing blog published by the National Council of Teachers of English (NCTE) and written by NCTE staff and members at every grade level from preK through college. The blog is diverse in both focus and content. Some of the posts explore classroom practices shaped by anecdotal experiences, while others favor the precise, academic style of writing grounded in research. Regardless of the author or the content, there is plenty of strong material that can improve your classroom instruction.

Moving Writers
https://movingwriters.org/

Moving Writers is a well-designed blog focused on the craft of improving writing instruction and, in general, on strong teaching practices that can be adapted for a variety of grade levels. Similar to *Two Writing Teachers, Moving Writers* has grown so much over the years that multiple contributing writers post multiple times per week. These short posts are quick reads that offer something new to consider while also humanizing the writers' academic experiences. One of the growing hallmarks of *Moving Writers* is its approach to writing over the summer, which involves the *Moving Writers* community in creating the prompts that drive a collaborative writing conversation for 100 days over the summer. This challenge encourages teachers—and anyone who is willing to participate—to write daily over the summer, sharing their writing with others in the community. *Moving Writers* not only supports teachers across the country but actively invites them to participate in writing as well.

Teachers, Profs, Parents: Writers Who Care

https://writerswhocare.wordpress.com/

Teachers, Profs, Parents: Writers Who Care is a peer-reviewed blog that emphasizes strong writing instruction across all grade levels. Two of its hallmarks are the diversity of author roles and the direct implications of implementing writing strategies that have been suggested in brief posts. Many posts feature hyperlinks and images. The editorial team behind *Writers Who Care* invites readers to submit work about the way they use writing or writing instruction and provides specific feedback that both challenges and encourages the poster in ways that ultimately help build the writer. Contributors gain valuable experience working through the publishing process in ways that mimic that of standard academic journals—working through drafts with an editor, including communicating with the editor and implementing feedback from multiple reviewers. Consider sharing some of the great writing instruction happening in your class with the WWC community.

Two Writing Teachers

https://twowritingteachers.org/

Two Writing Teachers is an aesthetically pleasing blog replete with ideas and questions that encourage readers to consider writing instruction focused on writers workshop from many teachers' perspectives. Because there are so many contributing writers, the blog is updated with new posts multiple times a week, which allows for a multiplicity of ideas and questions to consider. I found engaging their support for the growing movement of the teacher-writer by encouraging teachers to participate in their "slice of life" challenge. Essentially, *Two Writing Teachers* challenges teachers to compose a "snapshot" of their life and link it to the blog where others can view and comment. This activity not only enhances the teacher's writing, but it also positions them as writers alongside their students, perhaps even igniting similar writing activities in their classrooms. Overall, this is a valuable resource with a lot to offer.

References

Amiel, H. F. (1885). *Amiel's journal: The journal intime of Henri Frédéric Amiel*. (M. H. Ward, Trans.). Macmillan.

Applebee, A. N., & Langer, J. A. (2009). What is happening in the teaching of writing? *English Journal, 98*(5), 18–28.

Applebee, A. N., & Langer, J. A. (2011). A snapshot of writing instruction in middle schools and high schools. *English Journal, 100*(6), 14–27.

Atwell, N. (1987). *In the middle: Writing, reading, and learning with adolescents*. Boynton/Cook.

Birkenstein, C., & Graff, G. (2008). Point of view: In teaching composition, "formulaic" is not a four-letter word. *Style, 42*(1), 18–21.

Blau, S. (1993). Constructing knowledge in a professional community: The Writing Project as a model for classrooms. *Quarterly of the National Writing Project and the Center for the Study of Writing and Literacy, 15*(1), 16–17, 19.

Blau, S. (2003). *The literature workshop: Teaching texts and their readers*. Heinemann.

Boud, D. (2001). Using journal writing to enhance reflective practice. *New Directions for Adult and Continuing Education, 90*, 9–18. https://doi.org/10.1002/ace.16

Boud, D., Keogh, R., & Walker, D. (Eds.). (1985). *Reflection: Turning experience into learning*. RoutledgeFalmer.

Cameron, J. (2016). *The artist's way: A spiritual path to higher creativity* (25th anniv. ed.). TarcherPerigee.

Charney, D., Newman, J. H., & Palmquist, M. (1995). "I'm just no good at writing": Epistemological style and attitudes toward writing. *Written Communication, 12*(3), 298–329. https://doi.org/10.1177/0741088395012003004

Christensen, L. (2017). *Reading, writing, and rising up* (2nd ed.). Rethinking Schools.

Cochran-Smith, M., & Lytle, S. L. (1992). *Inside/outside: Teacher research and knowledge*. Teachers College Press.

Cochran-Smith, M., & Lytle, S. L. (1999). Relationships of knowledge and practice: Teacher learning in communities. *Review of Research in Education, 24*(1), 249–305.

Cochran-Smith, M., & Lytle, S. (2001). Beyond certainty: Taking an inquiry stance on practice. In A. Lieberman & L. Miller (Eds.), *Teachers caught in the action: Professional development that matters* (pp. 45–58). Teachers College Press.

Cochran-Smith, M., & Lytle, S. (2009). *Inquiry as stance: Practitioner research for the next generation*. Teachers College Press.

Dean, D. (2008). *Genre theory: Teaching, writing, and being*. National Council of Teachers of English.

Desimone, L. M. (2011). A primer on effective professional development. *Phi Delta Kappan, 92*(6), 68–71. https://doi.org/10/gfw2mj

Duckworth, A. (2016). *Grit: The power of passion and perseverance* [Audiobook]. Scribner.

Dweck, C. S. (2006). *Mindset: The new psychology of success*. Random House.

Dyson, A. H. (1993). Negotiating a permeable curriculum: On literacy, diversity, and the interplay of children's and teachers' worlds. *NCTE Concept Papers, No. 9*. National Council of Teachers of English.

Ebarvia, T. (2018, July 11). Disrupting texts as a restorative practice. *Triciaebarvia.org*. https://triciaebarvia.org/2018/07/11/disrupting-texts-as-a-restorative-practice/

Elbow, P. (1998). *Writing without teachers* (2nd ed.). Oxford University Press.

Erickson, H. L. (2002). *Concept-based curriculum and instruction: Teaching beyond the facts*. Corwin.

Fisher, M. T. (2008). *Black literate lives: Historical and contemporary perspectives*. Routledge.

Fleischer, C. (1995). *Composing teacher-research: A prosaic history*. SUNY Press.

Fleischer, C., & Andrew-Vaughan, S. (2009). *Writing outside your comfort zone: Helping students navigate unfamiliar genres*. Heinemann.

Gay, G., & Kirkland, K. N. (2003). Developing cultural critical consciousness and self-reflection in preservice teacher education. *Theory Into Practice, 42*(3), 181–87. https://doi.org/10/bx7spv

Goswami, D., & Stillman, P. R. (Eds.). (1987). *Reclaiming the classroom: Teacher research as an agency for change.* Boynton/Cook.

Graham, S., & Perin, D. (2007). A meta-analysis of writing instruction for adolescent students. *Journal of Educational Psychology, 99*(3), 445–76. https://doi.org/10.1037/0022-0663.99.3.445

Graham, S., & Sandmel, K. (2011). The process writing approach: A meta-analysis. *Journal of Educational Research, 104*(6), 396–407. https://doi.org/10.1080/00220671.2010.488703

Guthrie, J. T., Cox, K. E., Knowles, K. T., Buehl, M., Mazzoni, S. A., & Fasulo, L. (2000). Building toward coherent instruction. In L. Baker, M. J. Dreher, & J. T. Guthrie (Eds.), *Engaging young readers: Promoting achievement and motivation* (pp. 209–15). Guilford Press.

Harris, J. (2006). *Rewriting: How to do things with texts.* Utah State University Press.

Hillocks, G., Jr. (1984). What works in teaching composition: A meta-analysis of experimental treatment studies. *American Journal of Education, 93*(1), 133–70. https://doi.org/10.1086/443789

Hochstetler, S. (2007). The preparation of preservice secondary English teachers in writing instruction: A case study of three California colleges' education programs. *Action in Teacher Education, 29*(2), 70–80.

Holland, R. W. (2012). *Deeper writing: Quick writes and mentor texts to illuminate new possibilities.* Corwin.

hooks, b. (1994). *Teaching to transgress: Education as the practice of freedom.* Routledge.

Kinloch, V. (Ed.). (2011). *Urban literacies: Critical perspectives on language, learning, and community.* Teachers College Press.

Kinloch, V. (2013). Difficult dialogues in literacy (urban) teacher education. In C. Kosnik, J. Rowsell, P. Williamson, R. Simon, & C. Beck (Eds.), *Literacy teacher educators: Preparing teachers for a changing world* (pp. 107–20). SensePublishers.

Ladson-Billings, G. (1992). Culturally relevant teaching: The key to making multicultural education work. In C. Grant (Ed.), *Research and multicultural education: From the margins to the mainstream* (pp. 106–21). Falmer Press.

Lieberman, A., & Wood, D. (2001). When teachers write: Of networks and learning. In A. Lieberman & L. Miller (Eds.), *Teachers caught in the action: Professional development that matters* (pp. 174–87). Teachers College Press.

MacLean, M. S., & Mohr, M. (1999). *Teacher-researchers at work.* National Writing Project. (Rev. ed. of M. Mohr, *Working together*)

Moffett, J. (1968). *Teaching the universe of discourse.* Houghton Mifflin.

Palmquist, M., & Young, R. (1992). The notion of giftedness and student expectations about writing. *Written Communication, 9*(1), 137–68. https://doi.org/10.1177/0741088392009001004

Perl, S. (1980). Understanding composing. *College Composition and Communication, 31*(4), 363–69.

Schulte, B. (2014). *Overwhelmed: Work, love, and play when no one has the time.* Sarah Crichton Books.

Seidel, T., Rimmele, R., & Prenzel, M. (2005). Clarity and coherence of lesson goals as a scaffold for student learning. *Learning and Instruction, 15*(6), 539–56. https://doi.org/10.1016/J.LEARNINSTRUC.2005.08.004

Smagorinsky, P., & Whiting, M. E. (1995). *How English teachers get taught: Methods of teaching the methods class.* National Council of Teachers of English.

Stock, P. L. (2001). Toward a theory of genre in teacher research: Contributions from a reflective practitioner. *English Education, 33*(2), 100–114.

Stock, P. L. (2005). 2004 NCTE presidential address: Practicing the scholarship of teaching: What we do with the knowledge we make. *College English, 68*(1), 107–21.

Sublette, J. R. (1973). The Dartmouth Conference: Its reports and results. *College English, 35*(3), 348–57. https://doi.org/10/bbzdw8

Weaver, C. (1996). *Teaching grammar in context.* Boynton-Cook.

Weaver, Constance, Bush, J., Anderson, J., & Bills, P. (2006). Grammar intertwined throughout the writing process: An "inch wide and a mile deep." *English Teaching: Practice and Critique, 5*(1), 77–101.

Whitney, A., Blau, S., Bright, A., Cabe, R., Dewar, T., Levin, J., Macias, R., & Rogers, P. (2008). Beyond strategies: Teacher practice, writing process, and the influence of inquiry. *English Education, 40*(3), 201–30.

Whitney, A. E. (2018). Shame in the writing classroom. *English Journal, 107*(3), 130–33.

Whitney, A. E., & Friedrich, L. D. (2013). Orientations for the teaching of writing: A legacy of the National Writing Project. *Teachers College Record, 115*(7), 1–37.

Whitney, A. E., & Johnson, L. L. (2017). The persistent relevance of a writing process orientation. *English Journal, 106*(4), 82–85. https://doi .org/10.1007/978-94-6300-483-1_10

Yeh, C. (2017, April 14). Forget grit. Focus on inequality. *Education Week*. https://www.edweek .org/ew/articles/2017/04/14/forget-grit-focus-on-inequality.html

Index

Author

Anne Elrod Whitney is professor of education at Pennsylvania State University, where she engages in research, writing, and teaching to support writers and teachers, inside and outside of schools. She is a coauthor of *Coaching Teacher-Writers: Practical Steps to Nurture Professional Writing* (2016) and *Teaching Writers to Reflect: Strategies for a More Thoughtful Writing Workshop* (2019) and the author of *Inkwell: Simple Writing Practices to Restore Your Soul* (2021).

Contributors

Paul Allison is a teacher consultant with the New York City Writing Project and at Lehman College, CUNY in the Bronx. He helps to manage Youth Voices and NowComment, two sites that invite youth into digital conversations.

Janelle Quintans Bence has spent more than twenty years teaching English. She enjoys the challenge of designing meaningful collaborative projects centered on learner agency. She is an active teacher-leader for the National Writing Project, where she served on the Board of Directors for three years. Her passions are writing, civic engagement, amplifying learner voice, yoga, and baking.

Amanda Micheletty currently teaches at Boise State University after eight years of teaching amazing high school students in Boise, Idaho. She loves hiking in the high desert and reading just about anything.

Derek Miller teaches English language arts at Royal Oak High School in Royal Oak, Michigan, and he is a consultant with the Oakland Writing Project, a group whose support he values and depends on. When not teaching, he enjoys time outside with his wife, who is also an English teacher, two sons, and a dog. He has read some good books lately.

Jenell Igeleke Penn is a clinical assistant professor of multicultural and equity studies in education and the assistant director of teacher education in the Department of Teaching and Learning at The Ohio State University. Previously, she taught secondary English language arts for nine years and served as the program manager for the department's English Education and Social Studies Education programs. Her research interests center on how nurturing spaces and visibility in the areas of pedagogy and curriculum help Black teachers and youth to experience and share affirmation, community, joy, and liberation. In addition to her research, she cochairs the annual Equity and Diversity Educator Conference at The Ohio State University and co-facilitates book clubs and programming for youth in local school districts. In her free time, Penn enjoys listening to audiobooks and spending time with her family.

David Premont is a visiting assistant professor in English education at Purdue University. His research examines how English teachers negotiate their personal writing experiences as pedagogical strategies in the secondary classroom.

Lyschel Shipp is an educator of English literature and composition. She is a writer, a poet, and a lover of people and languages. She is an advocate of the kind of teaching that affirms and acknowledges the identities and experiences of all students.

Paula Uriarte teaches at Capital High School in Boise, Idaho. A teacher for thirty years, she also is a teacher-leader with the Boise State Writing Project and was named a past Teacher of the Year by the Idaho Council of Teachers of English.

This book was typeset in Janson Text and BotonBQ by
Barbara Frazier.

Typefaces used on the cover include American Typewriter,
Frutiger, and Formata.

The book was printed on 50-lb. White Offset paper by
Seaway Printing Company, Inc.